# Lily Poetry Review

Volume 1 Issue 2

**EDITOR-IN-CHIEF**
Eileen Cleary

**ASSOCIATE EDITOR**
Christine Jones

**CONTRIBUTING POETRY EDITORS**
Suzanne Mercury    Lisa Sullivan

**FLASH FICTION EDITORS**
Mark Jednaszewski    Sarah Walker

**ART EDITOR**
Pamela Gemme

**GRAPHIC DESIGNER**
Martha McCollough

**MEDIA AND EVENTS**
Rebecca Connors

**READERS**
Kay Bell, Julie Cyr, Konner Jebb, Elizabeth Mercurio, Chell Nevarro,
Tzynya Pinchback, Renuka Raghavan Anastasia Vassos

© 2019. All rights reserved. This material may not be published, or reprinted without the express consent of the authors or artists attributed here.

# A Letter from the Editor

Dear Readers,

Steven Cramer asks in his contributing poem, *"Argumentum Ad Lapidem While on An Elliptical,"* Can anyone tell wisdom from despair? Our summer issue confronts this question with its collection of reflective poems and short stories. They take on somber topics such as illness and death, also curious subjects such as a Liddy Dole Sweater.

While curating this collection, we found threads that organically spoke to one another. Robert Wilson's poem, "Wooley Bears," answers Cramer's question: *They believe in healing at a distance,/that one day, a body synonym/will quietly take their place.* Sarah Dickerson Snyder's poem "Inside Sorrow," asks the reader to consider *the other word—pain,/the deep stitch that enters/ in the knowing you will die.* Beth Konkoski gives us a look inside a five-year old's view of her newborn brother's death, and *the hot, grown-up smell* of her father's words.

When selecting among hundreds of submissions, we look for writing that will ask our readers to feel beyond what's on the page. We're fortunate to have an exceptionally talented pool of contributors. Sometimes, we opt to host a suite of poems which allows the reader to get a more in-depth read on a single author. We hope you enjoy the collections by Wendy Drexler and Vera Kroms.

We're also thrilled to support young emerging voices such as fourteen-year-old Ashley Rensaleer who writes of how it feels when coming-of-age in "Waiting to Be Filled."

Summertime is often reminiscent of beach vacations, longer days, and warm fire-fly nights, but as these poems reveal, we read for the issue through the winter. We invite you to search for the wisdom in these poems, to feel the despair, and the hope. We recommend *Lily Poetry Review* for your summer reading list.

Enjoy!

With Appreciation,

Eileen Cleary

# CONTENTS

| | | |
|---|---|---|
| Eileen Cleary | Letter from the Editor | iii |
| Suzanne Edison | The Face of It | 1 |
| Bianca Rivetti | Drowning Waves | 2 |
| Elizabeth Mercurio | Camille Claudel at the Museum of Paris | 3 |
| | Inward | 4 |
| Andy Smart | This is | 5 |
| Karen Friedland | Babies in Jam Jars | 6 |
| Sarah Dickenson Snyder | An Index of Sorrow | 7 |
| Clinton Inman | Window View | 8 |
| | Theme in Red | 9 |
| Melissa Silva | Home | 10 |
| Jennifer Lothrigel | Merge | 11 |
| Anton Yakovlev | Sometimes Your Name Appears on Random Paintings | 12 |
| | The Minimalist Muzak | 13 |
| Anastasia Vassos | On Thira | 14 |
| Paula Kaufman | The Way | 15 |
| Ann Keniston | The Forger Recalls His Dreams | 16 |
| Steven Riel | New School | 17 |
| | In My Liddy Dole Sweater | 19 |
| Kelly Scranton | Type to Enter a Caption | 21 |
| Patricia Hale | Small Portrait in a Vast Landscape | 22 |
| Kevin Mclellan | Littoral | 23 |
| Jessica Walsh | Archeopteryctical | 24 |
| Mercedes Lawry | Green Curtains | 25 |
| Beth Konkoski | Brother | 26 |
| Mary Lou Buschi | Spring 1 | 28 |
| Mary Ann Honaker | Gwen Arrives | 29 |
| | Gwen and Rodney | 30 |

| | | |
|---|---|---|
| Marjorie Maddox | Chopping Block | 31 |
| Robbie Gamble | Boston Molasses Flood | 32 |
| Robert Wilson | Wooley Bears | 36 |
| Simon Anton Nino Diego Buena | Surface | 37 |
| Carol Berg | Origin Story: Fairy Tale | 38 |
| | Origin Story: Home | 39 |
| Ben Sloan | Snow | 40 |
| Ann Taylor | Grounded | 41 |
| Ace Boggess | Gastroenterologist | 42 |
| | In Memoriam | 42 |
| Lori Desrosiers | if i should sleep with a lady called death | 44 |
| Matt Stevenson | Ms. Wanda | 45 |
| Carine Topal | He Held me Bone-tight. He Held me Backward. | 46 |
| Sandy Coomer | Inside a Tulip | 47 |
| Natasha King | the geminids | 48 |
| Nancy McNally | Taxidermist | 49 |
| Andrew Gudgel | Muztagh Ata, October of No Particular Year | 50 |
| Yoni Hanner Kossoy | How Long Were They Honking? | 51 |
| | Greetings from Planet e, Forty Light Years Away | 52 |
| | Evening Prayer at Shaarei Tzedek Hospital | 53 |
| Libby Maxey | Farm Museum, Flax Country | 54 |
| | a reverence before the chainsaws start | 55 |
| Eileen Cleary | Review: To Love the River by Siham Karami | 56 |
| Erik E Hyett | Review: WORKaDay by Grey Held | 58 |
| Jennifer Martelli | Review: These Many Rooms by Laure-Anne Bosselaar | 61 |
| Michael Mercurio | Review: Destierro Means More than Exile by Maria Luisa Arroyo | 64 |

| | | |
|---|---|---|
| Christine Jones: | Review: Little-Known Operas by Patrick Donnelly | 68 |
| Susan Rich | Huge Atlas Incantation | 71 |
| | Medina Morning | 72 |
| Wendy Drexler | little prayer for healing | 74 |
| | The Gannets at Cape St. Mary's, Newfoundland | 75 |
| | Winter Ghazal | 76 |
| | At Great Meadows Wildlife Refuge | 77 |
| | Visiting a Friend in Hospice | 78 |
| Lori Slavin | Circus | 79 |
| Vera Kroms | The Queen of Hearts Testifies | 80 |
| | Mock Turtle, In Mourning | 81 |
| | White Rabbit, in Woe | 82 |
| | The March Hare Spills | 83 |
| | Dormouse, Afterwards | 84 |
| Rebecca Connors | The Coming of the Animals | 85 |
| Elisabeth Weiss | The Weight of Air | 87 |
| Margot Wizansky | The Reign of her Dying | 88 |
| Lisa Desiro | Slow Faults That Kill | 89 |
| Avi Prager | Gel Pen Hymn | 90 |
| Ashley Renselaer | Waiting to be Filled | 92 |
| Jenny Grassl | World's End and Ours And Why it Began Again | 93 |
| Barbara Siegel Carlson | Joseph Cornell Tries to Explain | 94 |
| Art Zilleruelo | You Say Obsessive Compulsive | 95 |
| Ocllo Mason | Movement and Color 4870 | 97 |
| Rukhsar Palla | First Month of Winter in Grenoble | 98 |
| Steven Cramer | Argumentum Ad Lapidem While on an Elliptical | 99 |
| | In Dundedin | 101 |

| | |
|---|---|
| Contributors notes | *notes i* |

SUZANNE EDISON

**The Face of It**

In dying
my husband doesn't wear
a death mask;

think of the rock aster's center,
its petals plucked,
the spiral of harmonies hovering

close to the ground. Some days
he's fog-bound and I play him recordings
of canyon wrens, their mating trills

cascade, reminding us of plateaus
and scoured cake-layers, of iron
pressed lime and sand, lichen fuzz-

whiskers on stone.
I remember his once, long strides
drawing him far ahead.

We used to imagine
we were early explorers, startled,
like grouse flushed from sage,

by the sudden yawn
of plunging crevasses, speechless
as fire ants but just as sharp, living

then as now, in wide-open territory.

BIANCA RIVETTI　　**Drowning Waves**

ELIZABETH MERCURIO

## Camille Claudel at the Museum in Paris

Her face pale, in a dark dress. Sculptor
       hands, idle in her lap. Sculptor hands,

with no clay to tempt them. The delicate girl her hands made.
       She caressed, and caressed —to make a girl.

Whose face I long to touch. Whose face
       reminds me —

Her mother denied her release.
       The mother who never kissed her.

Thirty years in an asylum.

Camille, whose face I long to touch.
       Her gaze, my own.

ELIZABETH MERCURIO

## Inward

I wake on the tile floor — face flushed.

Gardenias.     I smell gardenias,

like the kind my favorite teacher brings to school

and floats in clear bowls.

Angry, the nurse helps me back to bed.
    *If I can't trust you,*
    *I'll tie on the restraints.*

I can't explain why I failed, how I managed
    to push those pills past the tongue's fight.
    I need to keep my legs from shaking
    on the green gurney.

        Ringing ears, different voices,
        the same question —
        *why would a pretty girl like you do this?*

I stay silent

rub my fingers over the thin gown

just between my ribs —

where an orange-red terror bird twists from my heart.

I slip inward —
    no longer afraid,
        almost buried.

ANDY SMART

**This Is**

a doe eating my father's casketpiece. A tongue.
Ticks marching hinderquarter to neck.
Summer still. Tomorrow, summer.
Malaise of sunset bifurcating headstones.
Grassblades folding under hooves. A hacksaw
played with a bow. Forget-me-not, stargazer, baby's breath.
Footsteps walking away. Mother, crying away
while my father's aftershave fades. Gravedigger's
beat-up pick-up heavy on its springs.
He loads his last shovel in.

KAREN FRIEDLAND

**Babies in Jam Jars**

It's an ark of sorts,
this old wooden house,
adrift on the blue of the world,

with two cats, two dogs, two humans—
only we're all fixed or middle-aged,
so, there'll be no reproducing,

save for the myriad plants
which have multiplied
many times, over—

my babies in jam jars
by the kitchen window
that I keep trying to give away.

SARAH DICKENSON SNYDER

**An Index of Sorrow**

First, borrow the other word—pain,
the deep stitch that enters

in the knowing you will die.
Dogs and cats and squirrels

dig and eat and sleep unburdened.
Next, get closer to the surface

with the sting of unloved—
the one you wanted

who didn't want you,
who sentenced you

to heavy wings.
A shame—that hovers

and wraps its molecules,
no matter the thrashing

and rearranging you do
to displace what you know

to be true—a cloud
almost seen through.

CLINTON INMAN                                            **Window View**

CLINTON INMAN **Theme in Red**

MELISSA SILVA

**Home**

When I was five, I watched my brothers build a snowy mound in the schoolyard. I imagined an igloo home – ice stairs, ice bed, ice pillows. I ran to my house to pack my round yellow suitcase, decorated with a dancing bear. I put in underwear, a lilac crinoline dress, and Raggedy Ann. In the kitchen, I told my mother, "I'm going to live in an ice home." When I got back to the schoolyard, my snow house was smashed to the ground.

North, late December
Sharp snap of a tree branch
Suddenly the dark

JENNIFER LOTHRIGEL  **Merge**

ANTON YAKOVLEV

## Sometimes Your Name Appears on Random Paintings

The city drips like honey onto maps.
The quiet whoosh is different from dying.
Wings rain on us like yellow silhouettes,
silhouettes of time against the wall.
I tried to build a buffer from your bones
but knew you'd never understand. Truth is
a picture: naked, moderately guilty.
God pollinates the flowers the bees forgot.

ANTON YAKOVLEV

## The Minimalist Muzak

I take the elevator down into a drawing of my own life.
The minimalist muzak creaks like a shallow grave.
Back when you liked the colors of my shirts,
I liked being parked on the side of the highway with you.

Now all my shirts are ugly, so I drive you to your apartment.
Our talk is small. We won't discuss the time
our tortures sounded similar enough to church bells
for us to get married. Let sleeping dogs shut up.

The garden is a beating heart, but so is the desert, and I
was the nobody you wrote about. You take the elevator
up to your grave apartment while I linger in the mud
eating the offspring of your birthday cakes.

It's not your birthday, and I don't want to remember you,
but somehow you woke up the entire animal shelter.
Someone said you were moving up in the world.
The muzak was so strange you forgot to be angry.

We tried to visit every friendly face on the island,
but our third meaning must have gotten overexposed.
Everything is clearer with the highway empty.
Everything was parked by our side. Where did it go?

ANASTASIA VASSOS

## On Thira

On this island ringed in blue and dust
we climb ghost steps leading up,
out of the cauldron.

A widow dressed in black
guards the church.

Here at the edge of the Aegean
she tells us
there's more wine than water,
more churches than houses
more donkeys than people.

Feed me a country that curves
rogue waves round its edge,
then returns them.
I thirst. I hunger.

Baffled crater!
*Caldera. Caldaria.*
Language laces my Greek tongue
with the lips of a Spaniard.

We're at the hem
of the volcano.
I lift my dress,
the breeze on my legs.

PAULA KAUFMAN

**The Way**

A town famous for eyeglasses, silk.
The Ohara brush-maker has a ten-generation smile,
tweezes fur into bamboo handles.
Fukui sap flows from urushi.
Lacquer brushed atop abalone, quail eggshell inlay.
The emperor's craftsman only uses brushes
made from the hair of pearl divers,
who have never used shampoo.

In Kanazawa, kinpaku pounded whisper light.
Shimmer brushed atop cake, tea,
even ice cream ribbed in gold.

Who will continue making paper strong
enough for windows
next year and the year after?
Sift hand? Shake screen?
Elder drips paint, rings quiver out.
He is a ningen kokuho,
National Living Treasure.

My friends believe in the old way,
return home to take up tradition.
Unshoulder pack, squeeze trowel, swish, swish.
Plaster their walls in earth colored
sumi ink and persimmon juice.
Fingers uncurl from tile-cutter for tea,
to observe plum blossom.
They name their guest house Karigane—
for the goose who returns home.

*Kinpaku:* Gold leaf famous in Kanazawa city
*Washi:* Handmade paper made famous in Echizen
*Machiya:* Traditional wooden townhouses once found in abundance in downtown Kyoto

ANN KENISTON

## The Forger Recalls Her Dreams

Last night another set of stairs emerged as if to simulate some guiding hand. In fact, the brain's the boss of versions. It drains all danger from the daylit thing, invents a subterfuge that soothes. All night she died, and then again. Then she became my mother, who's long dead. I tried to hold her carefully. I brushed her hair. The stuck projector splits the scene to stills until the film gets singed. Meanwhile, off camera, more copies from the copier spew, each slightly less decipherable, though the selling agent sotto voce says: *Let's pretend this one's unique.*

STEVEN RIEL

**New School**

Banished: purple pants. Dumpster-stuffed,
along with saddle shoes with two-inch heels.
*Heels.* When I first came upon the pair of them,
spot-lit within the Thom McAn window for men,
I paused, anxious & transfixed,
two Saturdays in a row, drawn to all that suede
arches suggested
upon a carpeted pedestal.
I sported them the first day
at my first high school.

Couldn't have made a more neon
mistake. As I lowered my gaze to lines
dividing floor tiles, I learned
a face won't burn all the way
from Homeroom to Math class.

St. Jude, thanks for this second school,
second chance to get lost, blend in. Navy-
blue windbreaker, gray cords,
worn Keds. At home I practice
walking like a boy, aligning each step
along parallel tracks. I nest inside
a corner study-carrel, become gerbil
without squeak, scratch,
or telltale patter of scamper.

I shun other slouching misfits even if
at lunch I nibble turkey tetrazzini alone.
Too bad this new school's rules say
even Four-Eyes play sports after two o'clock.
My shins block kicks in third-team soccer.
Muddy, sagging pads almost cushion bone,
& I wonder if I'll always need a burrow.

Unnoticed underclassman
on a locker-room bench, I
don't let slip a mammoth moan
when the Varsity MVP strips down (*Good God*)
to just plump cockhead, its scrolled corona--
trophy-winning mousetrap--inches
from my enormous, untamable eyes.

STEVEN RIEL

**In My Liddy Dole Sweater**

I took Liddy out for her debut
in Houston at the Strange Door.
Entire agencies kowtow
to my fitted shoulders
when I cross the stage
in tailored herring-bone.

After shaving backwards
& forwards & sideways,
I Visine both eyes,
pulverize any mascara clumps,
screw on pearl-button earrings.

I follow her brutal routine
except she wakes up before dawn
when I'm slippering
my Size-12E bunions home,

but Tuesdays over toast
in her condo that I conjure wholesale,
I get all Big Girl Wistful
as I consider the Watergate pool.
A randy driver waits in the lobby
beside arranged hydrangeas.  Suzanna,
my Girl Friday, totes my slim briefcase.

I convene board meetings at 8:59 sharp.
A squad of lesser beauty queens
has the handouts binder-clipped,
my Powerpoint queued up,
talking points bulleted.

In lipstick this tasteful, I am confident
consensus will be won,
petty interests put aside,
the City upon a Hill rise up, rain-washed,
with epidemics quashed.

I can assure you that, like snowdrop blossoms,
segregation in Salisbury just faded.
No, I never paid much mind
to tailgate jamborees.

Once I've donned our Senator's lashes
I feel in my knees
how hard it was
to look pretty while climbing
a ladder in pumps
past preps at Harvard.

In my Liddy Dole outfit,
I toe-heel my Tri-Delt step across fairgrounds.
I nibble corn dogs without a smear.
I drawl back at my constituents' drawl.
I smile a genuine smile.

KELLIE SCRANTON  **Sabbatical**

PATRICIA HALE

## Small Point in a Vast Landscape

Late afternoon, nothing's finished.
I'm here on the back porch,

waiting for my mother to wake up,
or to not wake up; waiting

for the squirrels to leave the feeder
so the sparrows might eat their fill.

For the blue jay to catch
his balance on the roof.

Look at how he staggers,
wings too heavy for those frail feet.

The lights are on in the farmhouse,
and maybe the jay would like it there

where it's calm and still, no one
watching him through the glass,

no one calling others to the window,
crying, *look, look, that bird is falling down.*

The blue jay flaps his way to the feeder.
It's his turn. The old woman sleeps on.

KEVIN MCLELLAN

**Littoral**

The heat intensifies as Freddie ascends the stairwell and the suitcase become more unwieldy. He opens the letter outside his apartment door, reads "the biopsy shows no signs of dysplasia…" and places it under his arm with an unopened utility bill. He wonders what condition he'll find his roommates, the houseplants, after being away for a week and in this July heat.

Freddie undresses down to his underwear, tosses these clothes in the hamper along with the clothes in the white trash bag. The bagged clothes smell of ocean salt and sweat, reminding him of Dimitri from Thessaloniki. They had been inseparable. The last time they saw one another was in Dimitri's flat after he transferred to another London college in 1985. Freddie remembers his surname and can spell it phonetically, CATS-VOHN-AH-YOU-NEED-EASE. He wonders if Dimitri ever came out, if he survived the virus.

Freddie walks away from his computer and past the open suitcase, sees inside the rocks he collected from the Maine coast. He fills the kitchen sink about one fourth full with water and one at a time he submerges each houseplant. Each time Freddie passes the suitcase and admires these fist-sized rocks he wonders if Dimitri tried to find him. Angelwing begonia. Christmas cactus. Crown of thorns. Geranium. Green shamrock plant. Jasmine. Madagascar dragon tree. Orchid. Pencil tree. Philodendron. When the terra cotta fully darkens, he returns each to their respective post.

JESSICA L. WALSH

**Archaeopteryctical**

Let's time travel.
  You kill the bad guys,
  I'll warn the first birds.
Protofowl, neo-avian, my midway friend
  from scales to feathers,
I tell you
      you are to be Atlased
with Feelings     and if you are no messenger
      then messenger still—
most of us can't tell crow from grackle—
  We'll tie you lopsided with
our break-ups & heavens & deaths &
  old melancholy & dawn lust & even nihilist insomnia.
    (Just yesterday my daughter read "nihilist" aloud;
she is 11 and said knee-HEEL-east
  but got what it meant
    before I finished explaining.
        Wait, here is where you come in:
        I'll make you metaphor
          for what a mother feels
            when her child's instinct is abyss
              and the mother hopes she wings away from it--
    do you see how badly this ends?)
Better to consider yourself    already fittest,
  a finished creature.
  Try to keep your $x$.
If I go back to dinosaur lines
  then you will know for sure your purpose
was not sky but paper.

MERCEDES LAWRY

## Green Curtains

On the bedroom wall, a window, curtained in pale green. He is in the bed and can only see a thin slice of sky. The sky is sometimes a soft blue, sometimes sketched with clouds or muddy gray. Rarely, at night, a star will be visible in the slice. The air in the room is heavy with stink. He is unaware of the stink. When she enters the room, she is comforted by it. She does not enter often. At times she stands outside in the yard facing the window. She cannot see him, just the pale green curtains which never move because the window is never open. She'd chosen the green curtains years ago when she loved the man who is dying. He knows he is dying but does not know she no longer loves him. She is not sure where the love went. Perhaps buried in the yard beneath the hydrangea which he never liked because it reminded him of his mother who was cruel. She should have let him remove the hydrangea. It was such a small thing.

BETH KONKOSKI

## Brother

When Anna was five, she pretended to watch Belle in her yellow gown bring the forgotten castle to life. The movie, a magic dilemma of unruly furniture and songs, couldn't hold her attention. She was thinking of the new baby brother who was supposed to arrive soon. During her mother's final weeks of pregnancy, Anna loved to set her hand on her mother's stomach and feel him kick. She would picture him in there, tight and stretched, like a face pressed against glass. It seemed like days had passed at Aunt Mary's; finally, her father came and said this brother would not stay with them, *could* not stay because he was sick, like her dog had been sick and had gone to heaven.

"I can't even tell you how sick," he said, his forehead resting against hers until she could feel each ridge of the skin above his eyes. When he sighed, everything ended in a shudder and she smelled a hot, grown-up smell, like the diner where he sometimes took her for breakfast.

"Then Mommy will." She reached for his hand, his fingers thick and rough from the nails he pounded all day, the walls he told her about connecting together, until a house stood where it hadn't stood before. "It's all right not to know, Daddy. Aunt Mary says things take time."

So, she waited for the brother who could not stay, and she tried to watch Belle's dress twirl in a fog around her happiness. In the kitchen, Aunt Mary and the other adults talked over cigarettes, their voices prowling like cats. When the Beast on screen transformed into a prince, Anna's father kissed the top of her head and stood up.

From the corner of her eye, she saw her mother come through the room, a Bundle clutched against her chest, a secret to hide.

"How did you get here?" Anna shouted, leaping to her feet. She felt her father's fingers choke her arm and she dropped to her knees, slipped through his grasp. She dove at her mother, needing to hug her, to touch her, not just the thought of her. But her mother's palm met her chest, shoved her away.

"Keep her back," her mother screamed and for a moment, the blanket slipped. Anna saw the shadow of a face, a scrambled, mixed-around face like her Mr. Potato Head toy when she put all the pieces in the wrong holes. And then her mother pulled the bundle tight to her chest and rushed away, while Anna's father caught her in his arms, his palms tough and clumsy through the fabric of her nightgown. They landed together on the couch in a bear hug she struggled to break through.

Keeping her face locked against his chest, he rocked her while the voices of adults swirled in the room and the front door banged close.

"It's all right, it's all right," he whispered and continued to hold her as the house fell silent.

She could hear in his voice that he didn't believe his words. When she opened her eyes and was at last allowed to move out of her father's arms, there was only the empty room and the blank screen where Belle lived happily ever after.

MARY LOU BUSCHI

## Spring 1

Days before, we picked irises from the rectory garden. Seemed fair enough. The buds leaned in and out of the breeze—wanton little fists. Our 4th grade teacher was not a nun. She wore smart slacks, sweater sets, kept her hair short, made us stand at her desk recite the difference between there, they're, and their while steadying a mid-heel Ferragamo on her big toe. She never smiled, ate graham crackers out a baggie. She'd carefully tap each cracker before nuzzling it into her mouth. *It's opening!* she yelled. A quiet 4th grade watched a bud unfurl, a slow consistent yawn. We knew, we'd never again, see something this private, this small and strange, as if a tiny elephant balancing itself on a thimble was whispering into our teacher's ear, *miraculous*.

MARY ANN HONAKER

**Gwen Arrives**

When Gwen was born she was baked
in Earth's kiln and the wet whelp of her

slipped out onto the cracked ground.
Mother must have found her there,

Father tripped over her mewling
in the ferns while he tracked the cloven

imprints of stag.  Gwen knows this--
there are no photos of her like those

of her brother, his smushed grape face,
burritoed in fleecy blue, one twig arm

kinked out and blinging the hospital
wrist band, proof of human hatching.

Was her bald pate pasted over
with the gore of an ominous caul?

Did she wag a primordial little tail,
snipped off under the bright lights?

Perhaps sheened over with a silvery
mist of fur, a little beast?  Terrible

sharklike teeth to be shed quickly
in the coming weeks?  Profoundly

she yearns for such luck, such an odd
and precious spoon to smack her infant lips

around.  That there had been a warning.
That there's some secret to be found.

MARY ANN HONAKER

**Gwen and Rodney**

A clear strand of thought once unwound
from Gwen's head, fell on the ground beside her,

and morphed into Rodney the raccoon. Only Gwen
could see Rodney. By day he drifted around her

companionably, like an odor, and at night he liked
to scratch the cold glass of her windows, *screee, screee.*

Rodney's feet were magic and his paws left prints
of gold. He could walk his golden stairs into the sky.

Although he came from Gwen's head she was sure
he'd chosen her, only her from among all the children

who shove each other and squeal on the playground
and run and make up dumb games that all had one rule

in common: Gwen wasn't allowed to play, so instead
of tottering lamely after the others, conquering the maze

of the play-gym only to find on the far side
the children had long since scattered, and she stood alone

in the quiet gravel, Gwen walked along the far edge
of the field where cornflower, goldenrod, and

white and purple clover could be picked, where
if she squinted into the borderline of day and night

marking the forest's edge, she'd see Rodney sneaking,
peeking out from between the trunks to wink.

MARJORIE MADDOX

**Chopping Block**

Always, the raised ax:
shattered sky, steel staring down
wood and victim. The danger

of waiting for danger
cracks us all, each swoop
of aim and blade decades

in the making. This is the way
of memory, its ringed age
circling the foundation of trunk,

snaking the blind heart,
each metal glint refracting
the angle of fear that grips

its evening ritual
of chop, chop, chop
while a stranger —someone

like you or me— lies shock-still, face up,
and crows, those dark bystanders,
caw-caw sharp warnings of light

and fairy tales gone bad, even now
darkening into never-after; into forest,
into trespass, into now.

Open your eyes and breathe.
The night creeps close on dead leaves.
The hunter swings again his sorrow. Flee.

ROBBIE GAMBLE

## Boston Molasses Flood
*—January 15<sup>th</sup>, 1919*

1.

In the sweet deep of the tank
holding me, a bubbling up—
thick liquid char on flake of rust
heaving against steel bandings.

Rivets rack and complain. I work them.
Murmur, *Worry, worry, a long time*
*come now*. Then, leak through.

North End mothers send their kids
outdoors to scrape my drips off
into crocks to bake meager beans.

The company conceals
my dribbles with paint.


I am an umber column,
five stories high
two train cars across.

2.

Born of shackled African hands
sent west to the Indies
to chop, crush, boil the cane,

I flow into barrels
shipped northward
to New England colonies.

Then, distill into a grog for cargo
to be traded for more bodies

round and round the ships fly—
liquid, limbs, chains heaving,
the merchants culling their cut at every port.

I am the blood of commerce,
Sweet, Sweet Father of Demon Rum
a catchment, a wound
festering over centuries.

3.

I hear talk of a Prohibition,
distillery spigots cranked shut.
I am two million gallons backed up.

Do you believe I will evaporate
like that gracious vapor Freedom?

I lurk in pressured places
with the bones of all my ancestors.

4.

A midwinter thaw.
Warmth breeds, I bubble
and expand, stretch the bands,

and a rivet ejects from the tank,
another, another, then scores more
like Gatling bullets spraying the railyard;
the tank plates unzip, and I heave free
a great wave, viscous and falling,
forty feet high, a dark curve
eclipsing Commercial Street
splintering houses, gone
and more gone, elevated train
columns buckled horses scream
men look up mid smoke
women's skirts scatter
flying dogs, howl,
crash, where I curl
into carriages, gurgle
into pushcarts, lampposts,
downspouts, ooze
momentum squeezed

chest-deep into side streets
here a man     a horse     a child—

each a bubble hung above the lips.

ROBERT WILSON

## Wooley Bears

They pass for someone much older
carrying their soft caskets on their backs,
moving carefully so as not to miss
what they lost before: Tiger Wings
the consistency of whispers.

Children, unaccompanied, they trace
each letter with one finger,
sound out each word:
Animalia, insecta, taxon,
family.

Wooley Bears leave a third life
on the promise of a fourth.
They exchange their spiracles,
their setae's, for a paper womb.
They believe in healing at a distance,
that one day a body synonym
will quietly take their place.

SIMON ANTON NINO DIEGO BAENA

**Surface**
   —*For Tomas Tranströmer*

I moved: a trembling shadow
as lightning strikes outside.

Some houses stay lit
and this half-empty room,

a shell, that I curl into.
With antlers, moving

through fog and rain,
and a horizon of crumbling

monuments sinking
into the dunes, I filled

the blank pages with
holes, with my back

against the blackened wall—
that Neanderthals had left

footprints, in blood, all over
Europe; the forgotten

Fimbulwinter, now replaced
by ash—and the noise

I hear (lingering
ear to ear)

across the night:
orcas and the moon.

CAROL BERG

**Origin Story: Fairy Tale**

We were always children. Sisters who looked
like twins. Blond hair blue eyed, things

to place in a doll house, a little white box
on Meadowview Lane. The first sisters

telling tales to one another to explain Mother's
moving hands. To explain this neighborhood

of gigantic white tulips we slept under, tulips
like white capped trees. Perhaps we had become

chickadees and just didn't have the words to explain
our new white breast feathers. This thrust.

We developed like stuffed envelopes holding thick white
secrets, invisible desires in cursive handwriting.

The many meanings of blood between us.
We invent the words stars in sky

when really, it's eyes staring at us in the dark.

CAROL BERG

**Origin Story: Home**

The wet peach-colored leaves
of the dogwood tree, clinging damply

and then the letting go. The sky
before the first snow-storm,

all milky gray, sun diffused
as if hiding underneath a sheet.

The nuthatch spreading its wings.
Two deer in the apple

orchard, still, unmoving. Frost on moss
clinging to the rock—green ice.

Early dusk and the faint chirp
of the cardinal. A bank of stars

tipped white, murmuring near
the mountains who own their snow.

BEN SLOAN

**Snow**

*No one can explain exactly what happens within us
when the doors behind which our childhood terrors
lurk are flung open.* —— W.G. Sebald, Austerlitz

Prisoners in white-and-black-striped pajamas
stare at him through barbed wire as he trudges past,
a rifle resting on his shoulder to keep it out of the snow.
He pays no attention to them because he is hungry,
feverish, tired—a long string of mostly gagged voices
standing along a fence inside him, including his parents
reduced to the size of salt and pepper shakers
but still, though long dead, able to slap their son hard,
who, wincing, raises a hand to touch his smarting cheek.
He watches three B-17 Flying Fortresses cross the sky
on their way to Dresden. Blinking, wiping at his eyes,
he realizes what he never noticed before, that it can be
two things: painful pellets, so many tiny ice bullets, and
feathers rocking back and forth in the cradle of the air.

ANN TAYLOR

**Grounded**

Doctor's orders are to scroll
cursive abc's
with an invisible pen
between my toes.
Bored, I revert to
Whan that Aprille
and To be or not
thank Sister Anne
for making us declaim
To a Waterfowl from memory.

Ankle broken, foot stalled
on my hassock,
like the Christmas fairy lights
frozen to the deck rail,
I envy gulls' banking
across the solid pond,
while in drifts, snowbirds
stir up snow swirls,
as they must. And then
there are the bossy coots
claiming the only open pool,
and two puffed-up hawks,
side by side, sharing an icy limb.

Would that all this toe-ing,
could scroll me into a poem,
like Bryant's waterbird,
or that blackbird taken
thirteen different ways,
or even that bird simply
coming down a walk
or any other poet's bird.

I have the subjects.
I have the time.

ACE BOGGESS

## Gastroenterologist

Throat won't heal, I tell him—pointing,
shrugging, trembling as though
I've been sent to the principal's office
again. I already know

this man has no answers
any more than the women before
who thumbed my neck
as if it were smudged with soot.

He's paid to spelunk caverns of my body,
seek unusual formations, &
take photos: selfie with my peptic ulcer,
still life with small intestine.

I'm trying to sing a refrain,
forcing notes without agony,
but healthcare is a circle of uncertainty,
ouroboros rather than caduceus.

I'm hot-potato'd, passed around:
block print on charts.
Doctor, I need a lullaby.
Put me to sleep until the healing hour.

ACE BOGGESS

**In Memoriam**

In my mother's apartment after the divorce:
their corpses everywhere
seemed as though they'd skirmished
in the cockroach war—
Battle of Kitchen Cabinets,
fortified siege behind the toilet,
all quiet along the western floorboards.

There were hundreds no longer scavenging.
We kept a clean place,
didn't invite them in like witnesses
testifying to the spirit of some foul gospel.
The many stopped by one day &
died—apartment improvised as cemetery.

I return to that image,
not orange golf balls escaping the course
across the street; not my loneliness, self-pity:
cockroach cult martyred as by pesticide,
their messianic leader missing the point,
the route. We strayed among bodies
still & scattered throughout
our broken lives.

LORI DESROSIERS

**if i should sleep with a lady called death**
*—after e.e. cummings*

if i should sleep with a lady called death
get a dog to keep you warm
to take a ball between her teeth
(bounding pleasure everywhere).

Watching how the lithe form
of your body runs with her
doggedly, i will wish you every day
pocketsful of little tasty biscuits.

Dress her in stupid doggy clothes,
start wearing "I love my pug" tee shirts.
Understanding why her eyes bulge
i will know where any day

to find you happy on the whole
to find a simple life, a canine soul.

MATT STEVENSON

## Ms. Wanda

Sitting here drinking coffee and eating blueberries, it's a Sunday tradition. A hollow crow is perched on the porch in front of me, a metal one. The lady who designed and lived in this house put it there. Then again, it could be a mockingbird, but the thing is a foot tall. It's got a round hole right where it's natural hole should be. In the summer time, I like to watch the wasps fly every which way, coming in and out of it. A studio sits in the backyard, it's got a bunch of paintbrushes stuck in the floor. The lady was a portrait artist, which is a funny way of saying that she taught drawing at the local middle school. She says it keeps her honest and gives her strength and confidence, I'm not sure what that means. Pretty sure she drives past here and wonders what I've done to the place, what I've done to her hollow metal mocking-crow. I'm probably going to get drunk one night and crack that darn thing open, looking for honey.

CARINE TOPAL

**He Held Me Bone-tight. He Held Me Backward.**
*—Thomas Heise*

He hated the chairs with red satin cushions. He hated the cushions, the satin, the chairs. He cried blood each time he sat for dinner. Desire turned pale beneath our clothes. While facing the doorway he whispered in my good ear. I swallowed my luck, noticed the wounds on both his wrists. He walked me in circles, held me in a way that, given a few thin seconds, meant trouble. Afterward, I couldn't eat. For god's sake I shimmied to break free while winking him down. He said death has a life of its own. Until then, I'd been a good Jane in a tight dress. Adjustments were made.

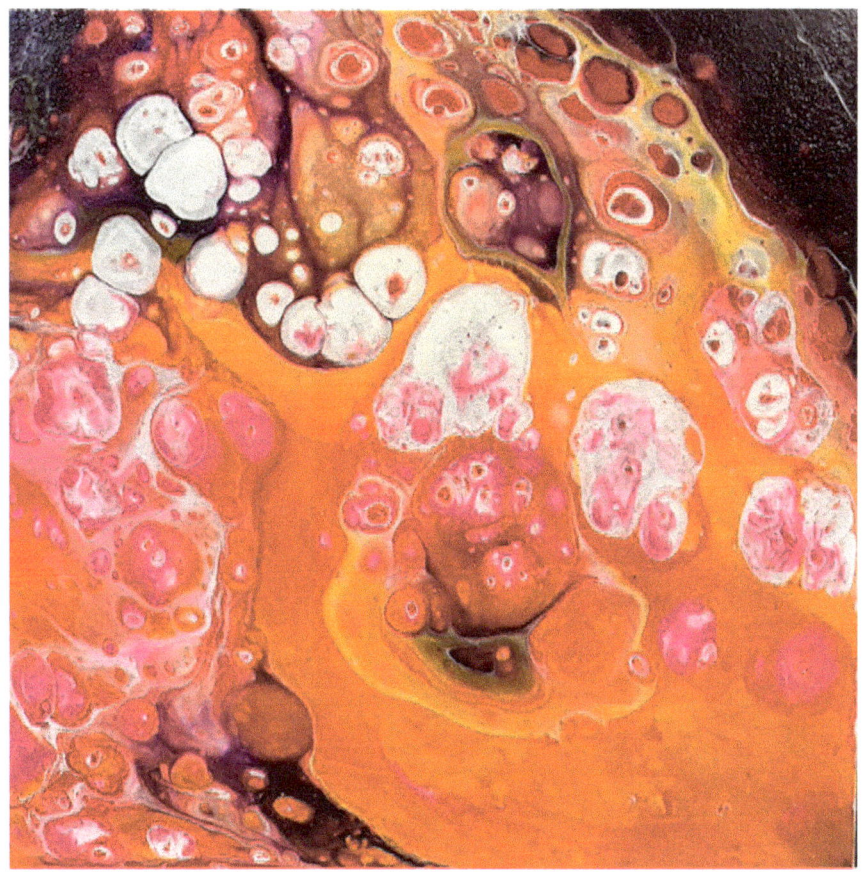

SANDY COOMER																								Inside a Tulip

NATASHA KING

**the geminids**

crosshatched under sundry blankets, my brothers and i.
watching for the minnow streaks of meteors.
having woken and summoned each other quietly.
in the dark, while our parents slept in their divided bed.
my brothers and i: tangled like nebulae, like star gas, like certain orbits.
cold toes tucked into the warm crooks of knees.
out on the porch under the dark cold face of heaven.
*there's one,* we said. *we see it, we see it.*

MARCY MCNALLY

## Taxidermist

zebra stuffed into apricot
sunlight, I walk into bones,
preparing a new myth:

Dusk of Animalistic Pride, my tribal ritual
becomes an eerie tribute to the natural world,
to the realm of survival, as I carefully dissect
the sinews and tissues, precisely mounting
each delicate element with wire strand and
cotton thread, as calmly as you once surveyed
the Tanzanian hills at the setting of a wild sun.

ANDREW GUDGEL

**Muztagh Ata, October of No Particular Year**

The snowy mountain peak crouches,
A mirror between its knees,
Turquoise and ivory doubled, inverted,
While caravan bells on sardonic camels jangle
Further down the shore.

The sharp, razor wind carries
Hints of snow and saffron,
Lost books, prayers in dead languages,
While the air-brakes of battered buses cough
Out upon the road.

YONI HAMMER-KOSSOY

## How Long Were They Honking?

I like how the guy in the dented van cuts you off and you let him. Shows character, as if you always prefer getting stuck at a traffic light to making a fuss. There's a song on the radio you haven't heard in twenty years so you belt it out, thumping on the steering wheel with every hook. And because the sun presses hot through the windshield, you answer its command to bloom in a riot of grasses and poppies as all rocky hillsides must. You say time is a capsule of seconds, thinking of a lost Tupperware that never completely sealed. Thinking there is no time, only days when the wind beats the city like a tattered rug dragged over a terrace rail, sending up great gouts of dust before rolling it back into place.

YONI HAMMER-KOSSOY

## Greetings from Planet e, Forty Light Years Away

good peoples
we hope this gets through
your news flog
in these low times
you are not alone
we too have small men
must make
ignore & the love
it's what must be done
we look out at terrible space
& envy your long years
your sun so ablaze
remember the dark makes way
for almond tree bloom

YONI HAMMER-KOSSOY

## Evening Prayer at Shaarei Tzedek Hospital

This is how it feels
to be a forest: each tree alone
within reach of another

each tree bent from holding up
the sky. Sometimes a great wind
blows and all the trees sway

sometimes there's a hush
and only one seems to move
from an unseen breath.

LIBBY MAXEY

**Farm museum, flax country**

After scutching came the hackle—
        a bed of nails.

In the house, spinning
        and winding yarn on the squirrel cage swift.

She was named Thankful
        so he could say it

when he came for supper
        on a cloud of unmade clothes.

LIBBY MAXEY

## a reverence, before the chainsaws start
*qui coluere colantur*—Ovid's *Metamorphoses,* VIII.724

witness the fidelity of trees
how the oak's November leaves
tossing at the crown like an auburn
swarm of bees hold tight
marcescent winterlong

and the linden every June
honeying the air unobtrusively
the scent of ancient Sicily abroad
for two golden weeks
for centuries

because Philemon and Baucis
shared this constancy in love and worship
Jove made them these
their branches twining
at his temple

such solidity is real and to be cherished
though my wood is full of fallen birch
and hollowed beech
and willow withies strew the yard
with every breeze

EILEEN CLEARY

*To Love the River* by **Siham Karami**
**Kelsay Books, 2018, $14.00**

Enter the wild and protean imagination of Siham Karami and grok that dawn "is a single hair edge from the deep" and "hairy night." Like any magical being, Karami inhabits and names the spaces that drift away from mortals. For instance, the poet builds a threshold where a woman can reach the little girl that the speaker's womanhood extinguished.

Karami writes in "Bird of Paradise:"

> The little girl who disappeared
> when cut off by her womanhood
> now rises like a phantom bird
> whose language no one understood
>
> except the birch trees and the wind
> and old chairs and familiar stones
> long gone, their traces in my mind,
> their words now marrow in my bones.

It is astonishing how Karami creates of emotion, a place. She demonstrates this in "Scarfish."

> I have no moorings in your sea
> And yet I live there anyway.

In the title poem "To Love the River," Karami leads readers to a darker place with Dickinson-like wrestling of death, nature, and even the universe.

> You wouldn't like how my delicate arms
> flailed uselessly in the rapids,
> of the dim green diorama
> of death where I spent my oblivion.

To Karami, poetry is music and as such is composed rather than written. This is most likely why common noise assaults this poet's ear. Karami responds by transforming this racket of the quotidian to a song called, "Mallwaves."

> Voices river through the concert hall
> Cacophony, a common vowel
> dropped like the gravity that binds us all
> to earth the static on the radio
> picked up from Jupiter. Somewhere in the wall.

This poet journeys from delicate arms to Jupiter, to oblivion and beyond and I am not surprised because I always find reading a poetry collection's table of contents predictive. If I wonder if I'll be drawn to a poet, a group of well-titled poems can pull me in. The title "The Word for Dawn," told this reader that Karami reveres language. "Out of the Dark Wild Deep" and "My Heart is an Extremity" said these poems are otherworldly and written with subconscious mysticism rather than rigid intent. "Scarfish" advised me to be on the hunt for creative concision and to expect some clichés to be turned on their heads. "Once Upon a Time in Northwoods, Minnesota" let me know that no matter how ethereal these poems may become, they remain earthly and can tell a story. This book is everything the table of contents predicts and more. To explore luminous spaces in the hands of this capable and imagistic poet is a true pleasure.

The verse in *To Love the River* is as diverse and textured as the life in any natural body of water. Like the life forms of a river, these poems are spectacularly connected to the energies around them.

ERIC E HYETT

*WORKaDAY* by Grey Held
Future Cycle Press 2019. $15.95

Throughout history, poets have performed all kinds of jobs in order to support their work. Zbigniew Herbert counted lice in a laboratory. Wallace Stevens was an executive at an insurance company. Grey Held's third book of poems, WORKaDAY, takes as its subject the poet's career as an international business development executive for Bitstream, Lyra and Forrester Research. Held thanks these three companies in the book's acknowledgements "for providing income and experience," but it's clear that the corporate world was no place for a poet of Held's moral sensitivity and clear artistic talent. This tension is what makes WORKaDAY so effective, and also imbues the book with a semi-pornographic quality, as though we are being welcomed into a rarefied world where poets are truly not supposed to venture.

I laughed out loud in "Casual Friday" where the speaker is trying to impress the receptionist during an office fire drill:

She's erasing

> her goose bumps by jumping up and down
>     all the while complaining about fake
> fire drills, fake bacon bits, fake
>     people. On the concrete sidewalk

> colored and molded to simulate brick,
> I'm standing, wearing my motorcycle jacket.
>     Check the label. It's leather.
>     It's genuine.

WORKaDAY explores exactly that conflict: the fake vs. the genuine. Throughout the book's journey, the speaker (Held, in the present-tense corporate version of himself that inhabits most of the poems) is agonizingly aware of the dangerous, sometimes violent insensitivity of the world in which he earns his living. Firing people (and being fired himself) is part of his job. His choices— the things he does to cope—are both heartbreaking and hilariously real.

As one would expect from a book of corporate poetry, WORKaDAY is beautifully organized. An opening chapter, "Upward Progress To Measure Like A Stock Price" sets up the book's psychic predicament: a poet trapped in the corporate boardroom, struggling impeccably with the moral expectations accompanying such responsibility. The middle four chapters chronicle business trips Held took during his days as an executive. And the final two chapters, "Re-Evaluation" and "Shaking Off My Expectations" explore some of the ways Held managed to reinvent himself after being let go, especially in a touchingly hilarious poem called "Fired" where he commits the perfect act of poetic vandalism.

WORKaDAY is a really fun read— fun, and agonizing. "Post-It Notes," which celebrates the small sticky squares whose messages represent the only signs of humanity in the speaker's office— is written in post-it note form, and is one of the best odes I've read in years. "Business Class" absolutely nails the elitism and false pride engendered by a premium seat on a flight: "I'm not ashamed," Held writes, "I'm MileagePlus // I'm Platinum Elite."

Held's speaker is a funny, self-aware, totally-believable businessman, who uses his corporate-sponsored free time to visit art museums, track down family history, flirt with women in passing, and even (on a trip to Germany) consider the role of his client company in the Holocaust. Held's speaker does everything right, and everything wrong: he loves his clients and pities them at the same time. In one of my favorite poems, "Kunstpalast Museum," Held, not knowing what else to do, buys a two-for-one crucifix bookmark for his customer. So much is at stake in WORKaDAY as Held's speaker struggles repeatedly to connect his career to his own family history, build authentic relationships with his clients, and finally to refine and develop his own, true sense of accomplishment.

My favorite chapter of WORKaDAY is "Business Trip To Richmond, Where I Grew Up." Held delivers a high-stakes situation: returning to give a presentation in his hometown. Coming after three chapters of elaborate, perfect poems about the bedsheets in five-star hotels of the world, the reader is suddenly presented with a well-defined understanding of exactly what demons Held is struggling with. In "Driving Past Kessler's Farm On The Way

To Richmond Airport," he remembers his teenage summer of Virginia farm work with a deeply-resonant nostalgia.

> Nights I'd sleep on a lumpy horsehair
> mattress in a room over the porch,
> my sheets coarse as feedbags.

> And wasn't I
> happy, so happy
> in the mornings
> to wake up and run?

It doesn't take a genius to figure out that the answer to the question is Yes. Nonetheless, it takes two more chapters for WORKaDAY to reach its conclusion, and for Held to leave the corporate world behind, taking with him a different understanding of himself. Based on this beautifully-crafted third book, it's easy to see that Grey Held actually was very good at his work in the corporate world. But Held's poetry is far too good for a world like that: every moment of WORKaDAY is completely believable; every moment of it, completely real.

JENNIFER MARTELLI

**These Many Rooms, Laure-Anne Bosselaar**
**Four Way Books 2018, $15.95**

In her opening poem, "Attic Room in Belgium," Laure-Anne Bosselaar writes:

>> Dust covers the window, but light slips through—

> it always does—through cracks & under doors.

>> Every day at dusk, the sun, through branches,

> hits a river's bend & sends silver slivers to the walls.

The poems in Bosselaar's latest collection, These Many Rooms, recreate a rhythmic walk from one room to another—not only within the home the author shared with her husband, the late Kurt Brown, but the rooms within the heart, the atria of grief. Visiting and entering these rooms—in their California home, in the hospital, in Belgium—require the pacing of the poet. We are reminded that this is a broken-hearted voice, but also a voice of a master artist. Bosselaar's expert use of the rhythms of the line mirror the laborious heft of simply breathing after loss. In "[Clouds heave]," she writes:

> Nights, I'd walk from the kitchen to the orchard
>> & measure it, one foot in front of the other,
>> head bent, toes to heel, heel to toes,
>>> whispering numbers.

>>> Thirty-four feet wide.
>>> Thirty-three feet deep.

>> & still no tears.

Bosselaar also the uses sound in a gut-level and careful manner—a way that only someone whose first language is not English can. A multi-lingual, Bosselaar, despite a numbing sadness, delights in words on the tongue. The images, which are visual as well as sonorous, repeat throughout the collection, so we hear the thud of "dust & dusk" over and over again, tamping down the "jacaranda."

> Three days now & the sundowner stubborn: a hot hiss
>
> in jacaranda. It's in bloom. There is no blue
>
> like this one, dusted by drought & dusk
>
> but flowering all it can—

Bosselaar delves into the mechanics of sound, how the mouth and the tongue react to grief. In "[I had weeded]," she writes:

> . . . . I had
>
> a knot of thistles in my throat,
>
> I couldn't swallow. Swallow,
>
> swallow, I'd say out loud.

I loved her choice of the thistle (which, like the jacaranda, "blooms" throughout the book) because one needs to use all the parts of the mouth to say it. It takes work to utter "thistle," which is a prickly, choking image. When the thistle is removed, the movement begins again, reflected by the scansion in the poet's lines. Read out loud the opening of "[for weeks now]," and feel how it mimics blood flow:

> For weeks now, no thistles in my throat.
>
> I clean & count & sew & write & rake.
>
> I walk the oceans hem & hum a little.

But where are these rooms Bosselaar walk to? Are they "the ocean's backrooms"? Are they in the heart? In Antwerp? California?

As I read These Many Rooms, I thought of the word "stanza," and how it comes from the Italian for "room." The rooms in Bosselaar's poems are airy, blocked by white space and time. A lover of visual art, Bosselaar brings light and color into these spaces, even the most intimate. In "Bedroom," the light "puddles over the old floor planks . . . . climbs the wall behind/what his place was in our bed, & glows there." So the rooms, while filled with dusk and dust, employ the light. Like impressionist painter Theo van Rysselberghe's cover art, Bosselaar carefully uses light to illuminate even the encroaching dark, for the light "comforted us: it hid our own darkness." Taking the reader to her room in Antwerp, Belgium, "underneath the chicken-wire skylight," she notes that Jews were

>   sorted, separated
>
>   beaten, starved, shot
>
>
>   in *Breendonck*: only fourteen miles
>
>   away from my white, lit room.

This is a book of rhythms and sounds. A book of "Him & me. Him & me." Like imagery in van Rysselberghe's "Big Clouds," the poems move across the white page; the words and images float on the tongue; the grief courses through the poetic lines. Bosselaar writes, "I think of you, love—search for you in each room / that breathes between me & dusk, me & dust." The experience of bone-deep grief is parsed out in heartbeats, in measured steps. We feel this emotion as a pulse in the line. "Some poems will never leave me," Laure-Anne Bosselaar writes, "their scansion the beat in my wrists & throat." These Many Rooms is a book to be read and re-read, a book I will be feeling for a long time.

MICHAEL MERCURIO

## Destierro Means More Than Exile
## by María Luisa Arroyo     Paperback $10.00

I was recently asked by a fellow poet who my "poetry ancestors" are — a provocative and endlessly fascinating question for anyone who enjoys understanding their own context, as many writers are. I don't know if anyone has asked María Luisa Arroyo this question directly, but I enjoy the notion that she would reply by handing them a copy of Destierro Means More Than Exile, as it is a tightly-woven collection of poems written to honor and remember those poets who have shaped her work.

Amateur linguist and etymologist that I am, even before I opened the book I enjoyed chewing on the title, thinking about the meanings possible in a half-baked translation of "destierro", recognizing that the prefix "des-" is equivalent to the English prefix "dis-", as found in distant, distinct, disengaged, et cetera, and signifying a separation. "Tierro" is clearly related to the Latin Terra, and in this case stands in for the idea of a homeland or native ground. So while destierro may be literally translated from Spanish to English as "exile", for a poet whose sense of self and identity is bound closely to her native land, it truly does mean more than simply exile.

In her foreword for this slim volume, María Luisa Arroyo explains the genesis of the book as being her participation in the 30/30 Project for Tupelo Press. I am grateful for her elucidation of her process, including the detail that she spent each of the 30 mornings in communion with the poems of the poets she wrote to — and it is to, not about, as we'll see; these poems are in conversation with their subjects, not examinations of the poet-as-object.

Of the 32 woman poets honored in this collection, I was familiar with 17 prior to opening these pages, and yet despite not being on intimate terms with the works of poets like Catherine Sasanov or Magdalena Gómez, I never felt at a disadvantage in reading this collection. Indeed, from having read Arroyo's poems to poets whose work I do know well, like Ai and Tracey K. Smith, I was able to recognize that it is her great gift to share her love of their words independent of knowledge of their poems. Take, for example, this excerpt of Arroyo's poem ("Whose Hands?") to Diana García, a poet whose work I've not (yet) read:

> The video praised Hammond's genius, how he built
> a replica of a medieval castle, his home. Falso
> Mami said. Whose hands hauled the stone? Cut
> & laid each step for staircases that spiral? Plastered
> the cooling walls? Swept the steps for cobwebs?
> Whose hands built the air for echoes, cathedral
> ceiling, hollow walls for this organ's pipes?

One need not know the story of John Hays Hammond, Jr., the inventor whose home — christened Hammond Castle — looms over Gloucester, MA, to have a sense of the unacknowledged labor of those who did the literal heavy lifting to build this grand edifice. No, this poem builds our awareness through a list of questions about the details of building and keeping such an enormous house. It also does this, almost imperceptibly, through the repeated use of sonic affinities, like the assonance, consonance, and alliteration in "Swept the steps for cobwebs?" — a beautiful line for such an unbeautiful task. Arroyo's craft enables her to unfurl the meaning through image and action, to reveal how big names can (and do) obscure the work that constructed and sustains our legends. There is enough in this poem to open the door to Diana García, to stoke my curiosity about her work and how this relates, to have a sense of what Arroyo has learned from her poems.

It is with this sensitivity that Arroyo's poems invoke their muses, never descending into parody or pantomime, and yet one feels the intimacy with which Arroyo knows their work. The brilliance of Ai, certainly among the great poets of persona and monologue in English, is recognized and respected in Arroyo's tribute to her, a ghazal titled "cruelty":

> In 2018, the youth rage against empty prayers, guns,
>                                  more cruelty.
> No place safe for children, for Black men. Our country, open
>                                  sore of cruelty.
>
> With this president, masks fall. The KKK, Neo-Nazis, white
> angry men march, their minds twisted to the core with cruelty.
>
> Trayvon Martin, Michael Brown, Renisha McBride, Eric Garner.
> Cops did not see the God in them, aimed for cruelty.
>
> Decimated by Spaniards, Taino traces survive only in maternal
> blood & words. Hurakán, storm god who roars with cruelty.
>
> In your poems, Ai, no angels, no wounded healers. Hurt lives,
> hate breaks, sex devours. Souls here? You tore out of cruelty.
>
> When the professor jokes that the hurricane has my name,
> I say: I have family there. Thank you for your cruelty.

I've reproduced this entire poem here in order to show the multiple layers of truth that coexist here, creating a rich experience for the reader.

First we have the dedication to Ai, the aforementioned poet of persona and monologue, whose subjects were often marginalized figures given voice through her poems, and with whom this poem moves in harmony.

Next, we have the form, the English version of the ghazal with its insistent refrain that serves this poem well in never letting us escape from the different intersecting meanings of cruelty. I've read a lot of Ai's work, but do not recall having seen her make use of the ghazal, but Arroyo's deployment here provides a cohesion to the difficult emotional content of the poem.

Finally, we have the poem's intersection with the speaker's situation in America in 2018, keenly aware of the vulnerability of those marginalized figures named and understood in the center of this poem, and of the speaker's own interaction with the professor whose "joke" cuts close to the speaker's heart. In this case, Ai becomes a figurative mentor, a strong presence with whom the speaker feels an emotional resonance from which she draws inspiration to respond — to speak truth to power.

These three strands entwine in this poem as a powerful cord stretching from Ai's work to Arroyo's, a linkage unbroken by insensitive "humor", just as the speaker recognizes the lineage stretching from the indigenous Taino people through "maternal/ blood & words" down to the present day, and the parallels in their decimation with the cruel and senseless deaths of Black youth, both those named in the poem and those who've died since. And, with the same unflinching instinct that drove Ai, Arroyo places these acts of violence in their context, laying responsibility at the feet of an uncaring, cruel president.

This collection is the work of a poet whose sensibilities are as finely-tuned as her language. Even when the poet to whom Arroyo writes is someone with whom she had a relationship in life (not just on the page), there is never a sense that she is showing off her connections, that she is marking for us the boundary of an exclusive club. "Unmasked", which is dedicated to the late Lucie Brock-Broido, begins with Brock-Broido's well-known nickname ("LB squared"), but that intimacy established, moves quickly to reveal the portrait of a loving, engaged teacher: "you flipped up my mask, asked/me to write beyond my eyes". And so we enter a poem that, inspired by Brock-Broido, shows an idiosyncratic take on her dense wordplay, painting a vivid picture through descriptions of action and senses beyond the easy visuals: "…eat kebabs, sip chai, sugar cubes gritted/between our teeth…".

One cannot read this collection without being favorably impressed by Arroyo's ability to write poems that carry such emotional freight without slipping into a sentimental mode. The complexity of these relationships is allowed to flourish, even when the recollections are fond. And María Luisa Arroyo makes smart choices in terms of form and language; her multilingual ear is clearly attuned to the musical possibilities of English poetry, leading to a collection of tributes that truly honor their subjects.

CHRISTINE JONES

*Little-Known Opera* **by Patrick Donnelly**
**Four Way Books 2019, $15.95**

A well performed opera is a feast for the eyes and ears, and Patrick Donnelly's most recent book *Little-Known Operas* (Four Way Books, 2019) is such a feast. Its richly evocative cover depicting Maria Callas' lush red velvet cape she wore in the Paris Opera's 1964 production of Vincenzo Bellini's *Norma* compels us to discover the emotions of a human heart beating with passion and pain.

Donnelly sings his heart out in his quest for understanding human relationships with rhythmic lines flowing across the pages. Emotion bares itself on this book's proscenium:

> The first obstacle that wind met was the top of a White Pine
>    in the neighbor of the Right's yard, which is shoved aslant
>       the transformer with a flash, killing the a/c for three days
>          and spoiling the fish. The Other White Pine, its mate,
>             (from "In which I explain why I set the fire")

There are the moments of stillness when he forces the reader to pause in the white spaces between the vibration of sound each line releases. And there is loneliness as found in his poem "Long muteness at 46:12":

> At 46:12 I'm still three so I won't hear it
>
>    for another 55 years, when finally
> *—is it day or night, am I alive or buried—*
> she opens her mouth

Also desire and joy as heard in "Goodbye, little table" at 02:15:"

> While we two were together
> we only ever needed
> one glass to drink from,
>
> she sang.

Leonard Bernstein called Maria Callas "the Bible of Opera" but Donnelly's poem "Callas vs. Jesus" insists *Callas has no Jesus in her.* Its previous line, however, says *Jesus includes Callas* which I believe also means Jesus includes Donnelly, and all of us if we will. Through Callas, Donnelly speaks/sings his prayers::

> Not your father. And again
> I'll cross the Alps
> On just
>
> My exhaled breath
>
> (from "Envoi: Callas and my mother say goodbye")

Though he writes, in "Blood Moon" *long-finished with The Church or churches,* Jesus plays a prominent role aside leading lady Maria Callas. Donnelly, through his poems, such as "I dreamed that Jesus bid me to go", enlightens the reader (and himself) that Jesus' presence is in a feeling not a structure of a church or organized religion:

> My dear, don't weep, he said.
>
> One of them began, "A bead like amber
> hung from pine"—so you may, he said,
> find my virtue glinting in the dust.

Donnelly competently hinges the book on these two figures, allowing us to imagine them as performers. And we, as the audience, seated in our cushioned seats, are all-ears, waiting for the shrilled rush of emotion against the composed presence of knowing, that despite the tragedy, somewhere and by someone, we are loved. He deftly crafts his poems, to question, to listen, to pay attention to the ordinary, and to feel the heartache that comes with being human. As in the first line of "Jesus said Don't":

> try to draw me into an argument
>      about whether fairies can be saved:

Donnelly's vulnerability is humbling. He wittingly closes his collection with "I told Jesus When I was afraid". He comes full circle with another religious image for the reader to envision, that of Duccio's *Maestra,* familiar to an image we see in his opening poem, "A postcard of *Christ Carrying the Cross,*" replica of the painting by Giovanni Bellini, circa 1505.

He's honest about his struggle with his homosexuality when he was nineteen "laid down on [his] face in front of the altar at All Saint's Church on West Fort Street in Detroit." We can feel the cold tiles he writes of, can hear the strike of midnight. And then we understand the plea:

> I told Jesus, for thirty years I asked you to send me someone
>     to love, and
> then Stephen came and we married, but we were old, so I
>     begged you,
> keep us alive, let us live a little longer.

To read Little-Known Operas is to enter many worlds—passing through Japan, Germany, Paris, listening to Il Pirata, meeting an American-born Greek soprano, viewing the masters of fine art, Shakespeare, learning much about something you may know little of—opera for one, but also Buddhism, Judaism, mythology, and a Spanish word *maricon* for "faggot". This book is an education, not only in the arts, and religion, but also in our capacity to hurt and to love. Donnelly allows the reader to delve deep, falling under the spell that an operatic performance will cast.

In his Notes at the end of the book, Donnelly includes a recorded conversation between Renata Scotto, an Italian soprano, and Albert Innaurto, an American playwright, from which his inspiration for his Callas poems are derived. Scotto, in reference to Callas, states, "We are spirit, and we are god when we sing, if we mean it." Patrick Donnelly most definitely means it.

SUSAN RICH

**High Atlas Incantation**

Maybe we eat too much land, too much sky,
scarf bowls of majorelle blue,

gorge ourselves on the cinnamon-creviced rock face
until tagine-colored mountains give way

to olive groves, to riverbeds of sand and brine,
to lemon-colored shoes on the boys we pass

as we feed off of the *melahs*, the ghost villages,
and a mirage of trans-African caravans.

We dine at the overlook on a dessert of nimbus cloud,
on the Moroccan light as it nudges second helpings

into our bodies, slips argon trees under our tongues.
What can we do except stand and stretch—

make a bit of room for another casbah
with walls of silk brocades, with to-die-for

cedar doors, and an upside-down boat—
inexplicably—dangling from the ceiling?

And whether we notice, we inhale the bone marrow soup
rising from ten thousand human corpses

once starved beneath these marble floors; we sample
the human flesh of severed heads on the ramparts,

the slaves for sale at the end of a pink frosted road.
And everywhere we look: men hawking baskets of fossils, of red stone.

SUSAN RICH

**Medina, Morning**

Past pomegranate sellers, past hand-pulled wagons
stacked skyward with North Africa's most delectable bread,

      past riads and *fuduks,* silversmiths and silk weavers;

past courtyard cafes, leather shops, past labyrinth
after labyrinth of glitter and glaze—we negotiate inner passageways

      filled with herbalists, spice merchants, motorcyclists

and a clowder of orange cats—until, suddenly, *L'Art du Bain*
materializes on a spot Google Maps calls: *Unknown.*

      Until the cedar doors open and we enter the sanctuary—

soap mixed from camel milk and night-blooming jasmine, almond blossom
and rose displayed next to jars of black gels and potions, *foutas* and five sugar
scrubs—

the scene takes our words away, takes the petrol exhaust from our lungs.

We sample each organic cream, each ointment and oil,
our wrists and arms slick with it, our earlobes and necks, dappled and dabbed.

      And when the beautiful Berber merchant comes back with cups of tea,

he notes our alchemy and offers the story of the damask rose from his city
in the High Atlas where petals spangle the streets, where married women rise

      before dawn to gather sand-colored sacks of blossoms which imprint

on their bodies, their bank accounts, their beds. He mimes how the queen floats
at the front of the May parade, the streets transformed into a souk

       of coral, and puce; flamingo, magenta, and the light pink fingers of dawn.

You are very welcome, he shrugs and slips small gifts into our bags,
shakes our hands slowly as we leave—

WENDY DREXLER

## little prayer for healing
    *—after Danez Smith —for Barbara Helfgott Hyett*

the magnolias have opened
their milk-white stars for you
above the shatter

and over granite and over
the smallest pebble
may the streams run clear

and where there was once hunger
let the deer find berries and bark
in this unfamiliar grove

where you trace the outline
of your body on air
to fill the reservoir
of your brand-new name

and when you find yourself lost
like an ant in the petals of the peony
remember your life's work
has always been
to help the flower open

WENDY DREXLER

## The Gannets at Cape St. Mary's, Newfoundland
*—for Barbara Helfgott Hyett*

Barbara says there are fewer
                nesting pairs this year. I can't see

      the missing, only the sea stack
swarming with thousands of birds, a fever

      of birds, pairs nesting on narrow shelves,
racket of wind-whipped screeches and grunts,
      the air acrid with guano.

Walking back along the cliff, I bend down to finger
        a broken shell tangled in caribou moss,

          tuck the pieces in my pocket,
      throw them away that night.

You can't keep
    every broken thing.

          I thought maybe the rock walls
could last. Stones fall, clattering
      against themselves, the way the heart

      of an unborn chick
              beats faster the first time
    it hears the family song,
precise lifeline of notes
      that chick must learn. I thought

          all birds sang for beauty.
    Not for beauty. I'll learn
to love them more for that.

WENDY DREXLER

## Winter Ghazal

> *Nothing that is not there and the nothing that is.*
> *—Wallace Stevens*

See how the water leaps and dances, gray-sparked in winter.
Is it to reassure us not everything grows dark in winter?

Love unties its knot, takes flight in any air or season.
Unbidden, birds leave before the broken dark of winter.

You broke my heart and couldn't say where love had fled.
Had it been starved, long underfed? It disembarked in winter.

Wallace Stevens's snow falls free of any human misery.
One must have a mind of winter to bear the bark and bite of winter.

From the train, I see a tall oak, with branches bare—
Oh, to perch there, perceiving all, the sharp-eyed hawk in winter.

WENDY DREXLER

## At Great Meadows National Wildlife Refuge

I've come for the red-winged blackbirds,
their *conk-la-rees* and crimson,
for the muskrat nosing the edge of the marsh,
all wet brownness from tapered nose to water-shiny tail,
and I'm here for the burst pods of milkweed
and for rubbing their shimmery insides to feel
their smoothness, I've come for the fallen tree
whose upturned roots are beyond my reach,
tendrilled like hanging gardens, and for the lichen
that burgeons staggeringly emerald all along
the trunk's flank, for these woods chock-full
of downed branches, broken branches, branches
entwined with bittersweet vines, I'm for
the pursed fist of swamp cabbage bursting
through muck and decayed leaves, I've come
to hand myself over to this hard and ceaseless work.

WENDY DREXLER

**Visiting a Friend in Hospice**
      — *in memorium Dorothy Berger, 1923–2019*

I'd wanted to bring her a technicolor sunset,
we'd watch it together, talk about the light
streaming through. But I've confined myself
to the customary good-to-see-you, as if
this were ordinary time, plentiful time,
yawning before us. There's no net,
only free-fall. Her cheekbones have sharpened
her blue eyes. Her face is as translucent
as Indian Pipes. Have you seen them,
those ghost plants that flower overnight
in the dark after summer rainfall,
shimmering unearthly, holy unclaimed,
pale eyelash of arrival and departure?

LORI SLAVIN  **Circus**

VERA KROMS

## The Queen of Hearts Testifies

Intuitively lethal, I was a prodigy,
        an executioner from birth,
dozing my first hour while mother
        lay colding next to me.

I have a calling outside the tides of female.

The puffed and bowing of my court
        are drifts of deer, their throats
        such useful targets.

Even a queen
        bears ten thousand sufferings -- the refusal
        of horticulture to breed a rose
            as bloody as I require;
        a torso-less attendance by a cat who grins,
            taunting and inviolable; dodos
        and incorrect typists; sleepwalkers;
            the inadequately attractive.

I have a lean vocabulary of forgiveness.

The nature of this world is the nature of me.
The easily erased who flood my gates are cured
        of their lives.

Not one whispers *butchery*.

VERA KROMS

## Mock Turtle, In Mourning

The ocean cannot love me
    as it did when I was bona fide,

schooled with the minnow,
    racing currents.

Now hooved and lowing,
    I am half-sacred in the East,

reshuffled as if cobbled
    from the broken pieces

in a child's toy chest.
    Pastures call to me.

When I became a new, an only.
    the webbing of my toes

was stowed away, my limbs drained
    of underwater tinctures. I turn

to history, which faces the direction
    I love most.  Cellos weep with me.

I have the consolation of arithmetic,
    the lovely manners of the crabs.

VERA KROMS

## White Rabbit, in Woe

It is the tick tock pouring out,
        that is unhinging.
 A heap of morning worry in my tea,
        pomade for whiskers,
a splash of talcum in my spats.
        Clock begins its daily scold
in the land of Her.
        Once She was digesting
famously, when a knave arrived
        one-quarter-minute late.  Her gift
 for pepper and dismemberment,
        was, as ever, punctual.
Appointed times outrun
        my rabbit feet, persist in leaving rude
remarks on meeting doors.   I have chased
        the upside down too long.  I yearn
for pickles and my belly to the sun,
        like Cat dozing in milkweed, like the girl
who followed me.

VERA KROMS

**The March Hare Spills**

I am an old breed of squirrel, dosed
        with carroting, sporting shoes of felt

and mercury. A chaste wedge of cheese follows me
        like a pet.

I wobble out for a slice of tea
        to where a girl, graceful

as a weasel, sits at the head of a table,
        the tremor in her voice demonstrating

how one suffers indefatigably.
        No one is politer than the walrus

who attends, delicate in his wrinkling.
        We lament the extinction of oysters,

debate how many smiles
        can a malice hold?   Riddles tuck

the afternoon  away to the final
        heartbeat  which I drag  at the end

of my fob chain. At the bottom of a sunless porcelain,
        a small mouse is singing opera.

VERA KROMS

## Dormouse, Afterwards

The table is a morgue of teacups.
    The sugar a disgrace.

Mindless as asparagus, the hatter and the hare
    lie face down, suffering
from what inhabits them.

The afternoon has been chewed and drunk,
    its buckled moments giving
like a broken girdle.

A child in pinafore jammed
    decorum.

Among the crockery, I pursue leftovers,
    tiny vacancies.

Those below notice must in turn
    notice to remain unextinguished.

I rest in mousenaps, heed a white
    rabbit polishing his little shoes.

REBECCA CONNORS

## The Coming of the Animals

Wolves saunter the sidewalk.
Groups of three or four nod

to one another, sniff trash
in the gutter. It's 4 pm.

A few climb parked cars.
Their claws, a tin can sound.

Every five minutes, a howl.
People continue to window shop.

Scorched circles
appear on the pavement.

A tiger's been spotted in a neighbor's
backyard. It hasn't eaten the chickens,

nor the mailman, nor the sun.
It is still electric. Pads

the patio, knocking over furniture.
The local zoo won't answer the phone.

Off kilter trees, squirrel-chatter
drowns out chickadees and blue jays.

The tiger, not interested
in the squirrels. The wolves?

You can set your clock by them.
The local naturalist thinks

of impending disaster,
like when a canary

keels over in a mine. Or when snakes
appear, laced from telephone poles

to trees & the hawks aren't hungry.
The pink squid in the creek

is dead. No notion of how
it got there. Its eyes stare

up, from mossy rocks.
Clear water nudges its tentacles

into a wave. Perhaps it knew
like the tiger knows,

home is uncertain, facts
can be denied. The wolves,

every three minutes now.
Why can't you hear them?

ELISABETH WEISS

## The Weight of Air

The first summer
I left my sweaters out
quickly moving squalls
wrecked coastlines
and altered maps.
No one was without risk.
Roof shingles blew off,
trees bent in microbursts.
Then the *Andrea Gail* sank
drowning her crew of six.

A therapist massaged my hands
warmed up the paraffin
called it barometric pressure.
The weight of air
washed up whole fleets
in downward sail
inside my body's curvature
that endless blustery season.

Nothing could bring my hands
back from ulnar drift
not drugs or love or the sound
of my own children singing.
At dusk I collected sticks,
built a bonfire on the beach
while stars lit a path
and the moon pulled the tides
closer in to the pit
as if they said, *I win, I win.*

MARGOT WIZANSKY

## The Reign of her Dying

Sometimes I simply sat with her
and rubbed her parchment feet.
Dying was imperious,
the hyperbole of it, the smell and utter quiet of it.
I needed it to be finished.
I wanted it to go on.

Death stripped her legs
and buttocks, ratcheted her down to bone.
Winter milked her eyes over.

Her beauty had been windblown
with a constancy of pearls,
a beach rose too thorny to hold,
and like plants abandoned, she praised me
and left me dry, praise she let out
the way a cheese-maker starts
with sweet, then sours and curdles it—
love and reprimand mingled.

LISA DESIRO

**Slow Faults That Kill**
    *after Sylvia Plath's "Elm"*

The elm was taller than our houses, but dead,
its branches barren except when filled with birds.

Starlings. They clucked
like hens, commiserated: *we are all maimed.*

How can we tell if it's fear or ambition rising
out of these twisted roots? Ragged wings

flap across the blonde, bloated moon.
Shifting clouds, shrieking wind, voices

seeking —*Where are you?*— sobbing — *Here
I am, I am, I am.*

AVI PRAGER

## Gel Pen Hymn

They drew the curtains
open, early, fast — the sun hit us
We crayoned an unkindness of ravens in cornflower,
    magenta, and fern

They said they would bury us in any negative space left
So, we tried to not leave any

Gel Pen scribbled hymns
Thank thy holy
Anoint thy vermin
Plant thy mistakes
Grow thy feelings

They caught us
linking hands under the table
They caught us
eating sour grass on the walk home

the weight of emptiness
drilled itself between my scapulae
after you were taken away
sure, late, slow

You remain
Unpicked poppies and Belly laughs
Maple candies and blue lipstick
You've become
The mascot of everything taken from me

Sun shines into my bedroom
Yellow glowing vitamin alarm clock
I have a set of crayons, 96 in a bag
I'll read the color names out loud to myself
    and pretend you are here
painting my lazy toes glitter gold

ASHLEY RENSELAER (9TH GRADER)

## Waiting to be Filled

They tell me my brain is being made
that I have years to go to be complete
that I use the word 'like' too many times
that my agonies are muse to garden weeds
that my exuberance lives on sand
that my desire's a Halloween costume
that I conjure up seismic waves
sitting amongst all these allegations
I watch how a willow tree grows out of my face
its branches stretch themselves from my hands and fingers
creating a hollow home waiting to be filled
And this nagging feeling of despair stands guard
Like when you know summer is over when there are no more cherries
Like that pulsing wait for the response when you know
you wrote the last word like hoping for chocolate
while opening a box of soap
Like pulling hungrily the petals of forget-me-nots
Like, like, like, like, like, like, like, like, like, like, like
Like almost there. Like if only.

JENNY GRASSL

**World's End and Ours    And Why it Began Again**

desultory bits we are          indistinct from sky humors          earth and its saw-edged star

conjugal dust          this          long after men and women could glisten          longer          love

since we embroidered the corridor          with us          when you fed my brideness bedrock

and clay          I stitched a blue of parsimony          a meal of lace          in a slow unbuttoning

of last celestial moments          a gentle null will touch          not you or me          but our wakeless

lake          symptom of zero          readiness without ache          the memory of a screen door

slam opens swoons and green ratoons          pulpits of Jack in the woods          loops

of railroads          widowed love and parrotspeak          murderous and luminous alphabets

BARBARA SIEGEL CARLSON

## Joseph Cornell Tries to Explain

I loved each bead with its hole.
Every Cracker Jack toy has a story
that whispered to me as a bookmark
in a dream, a place I could lie down inside
where the blinds have cracks
and moonlight whitens the floor boards.
Because each symphony starts
with the movement of an ant
taking its grain of sugar back
to its home in the hole between voices.
Under the quince tree's falling leaves
I lost myself, and my breath
couldn't hold onto or let go of the bodies
of the stars that tore through it.

ART ZILLERUELO

## You Say Obsessive Compulsion
## I Say Nine Trees Counted Ten
## Times Equals Ninety Trees

If I count nine trees
   I have to count them
      Nine times over again

So that my counting ends in zero
   I'm like my father
      Who had to punish

Each forkful five times
   Between both sets of molars
      And would scratch his itchless right hand

After tending to his itchy left
   After they took the left kidney
      He would shake with righteous thirst

For his lost symmetry
   How hungrily we crave
      Order where there is no order

Music in the wind
   Sculpture in the clouds
      Scribbles in the stars

We comfort ourselves
   With these orders
      Only because we know

We invented them
   The real orders
      Stay drunk all day in heaven

And we find the fake ones
   When we need them
      The hospital chapel

Stank like stale candles
   The bargain bin in the gift shop
      Overflowed with plastic angels

He died with one eye closed
   I couldn't count the lid up
      So I pulled it back open by the lashes

OCLLO MASON               **Movement and Color 4870**

Rukhsar Palla

**First Month of Winter in Grenoble**

I was exiting Le Drak Art (a frequented club, half warehouse, half wooden boards and spilled beer), approaching a parking lot filled with cars covered with snow. The cars were freezing and so were the humans, sharing their last minute spliffs. And then I saw him. Well. Not him. Them. I saw *them*. Between boys and men, lately my favorite find, when scruff is natural but maturity is not. A combat green-coated figure pelting snowballs at *un ami*. I could not help but shiver, *le froid* of Grenoble, France, coursing through my veins. I picked up a snowball and threw it, aimed *pour le premier fois*, and hit this Boyman, square in the jaw.

Manboy, Boyman yelled. He threw snowballs back, and I used a Volvo as my shield. He missed. Missed again. A slow rumble formed, not the Volvo, but the hum of laughter boiling in his belly, mine too. We approached each other slowly. Inching. Step, foot. There's a footprint. Dodge! Shit! He got me; snatched my jacket and propped me up between the Volvo and the hum in his belly.

He took his hands and rubbed them in my hair, down my neck. Snow down my coat. I did the whimper, *j'ai froid*, because he's stronger than me, but it's the schemish-kind of plea. It was the please have mercy, I came close because I knew you would seek revenge, but I wanted to see more than a hooded figure. I wanted a glimpse of your face, to feel the hum in your belly. He kept laughing that damned laugh. *Mange bien! Mange bien!* More snow on my cheeks, while one of his arms wrapped itself around my waist.

We made eye contact for the first time and I saw mischief behind his charcoal frames. Boyman's lips inched closer and I turned so that he met my cold cheek. We were cat and mouse; I didn't want anything about that to change. God had answered my prayers in the sweetest form, a mongled mess in my arms. *Come take this*, it said. And I thought, maybe this isn't God? I looked at Boyman again, he was still half-laughing, half-swearing at me. Definitely not God. The itch and the cold and Satan had all come together.

STEVEN CRAMER

## *Argumentum Ad Lapidem* **While On An Elliptical**

Per usual this gym day, the world is all
that is the case, unless the opposite's true,
and nothing is. "I refute it *thus!*" confuted
Samuel Johnson, booting a rock to rebut
Bishop Berkeley's equally entrenched sense
that while the world's foot gets past the door
via eye, ear, nose, tongue and skin, that self-
same world's ultimately nil. Yet, neither
is it snagged in a world-wide web of dream—
wrap your mind around *that*
                                                —or so he thought.
Who thought? I'm lost. I guess I meant
how Johnson's plea to a stone begot a new
iconic sound-bite certain to beguile his chum
and future profiler, Boswell, who loved him well,
as I do, especially for this diss: "be dull in a new way
and many will think you great." Love it.  But

how slavishly I brandish quotes:  that I dislike—
like playing dummy to your own ventriloquist;
like plagiarizing the smartest kid in the class;
like borrowing Diogenes's lamp, its sulfur
and lime wick aflame in secondhand bodhi;
like. . . now where *was* I?—

                              climbing
in place. Hearts run downhill in my family.
*Systole, diastole*—which is which?  Who wrote what
verse, chorus, middle-eight, or lyric, John or Paul,
down to the minutest riff—those I have by heart;
also, who played which Frankenstein, Karloff
or Glenn Strange. And yes, I know it's wrong
to call the creature by its maker's moniker,

but after all, the name stuck, and isn't that
what we want?—
       to pass on some baton
of renown, however thin, to our offspring,
coterie, hamlet, city, nation; or if we're biggety,
the globe itself. And yet, what good's leaving
behind a humankind of groupies, if in life
you couldn't pick yourself out in a lineup?

"You think too much about thinking,"
says a friend. He likes the Pointillist's dots
of blue and yellow. I like the in-between
green they collaborate to make. We lost touch
around the time my mind became my *bête noire* . . .
Speaking of, for the first time in my sweat-stained
rumination, I've looked up. All four monitors
simulcast our unelected bully holding hands
with the-one-shaped-like-a-gelded-panda.
*God help us,* I think, but my thought misfires.
Can anyone tell wisdom from despair?

STEVEN CRAMER

**In Dundedin**

Around the Octagon, people drink flat whites,
don't leave tips.  Kiwis pay a living wage.
As overseas as the jet-lagged get—winter
in August; today yesterday in the States—
we sit like silhouettes, here and not here.

Lifting her white shift,
she pisses in a store-front, perineum
aimed at the café.  In the book on my lap,
Leonardo's Vitruvian Man, his ideal body
squaring the circle; on our list of sights
not to be missed, blue penguins
waddling up-shore to nest.

Circling the square, her awful squawk
grows distant; comes back.  She raises
her shift right at us.  Hard to admit
our disgust reflex rises, like reflux;
harder still that she makes us feel
at home.

CONTRIBUTORS

SIMON ANTON NINO DIEGO BAENA's work has appeared in *The Cortland Review*, *Fifth Wednesday*, *The Bitter Oleander*, *Osiris*, *The Henniker Review*, *Chiron Review*, and elsewhere. I also edit and publish the poetry/art journal, *January Review*.

CAROL BERG's poems are forthcoming or in *Crab Creek Review* (Poetry Finalist 2017), *DMQ Review*, *Hospital Drive* (Contest Runner-Up 2017), *Sou'wester*, *The Journal*, *Spillway*, *Redactions*, *Radar Poetry*, and *Verse Wisconsin*. Her recent chapbook, *The Johnson Girls*, is available from dancing girl press. She was winner of a scholarship to Poets on the Coast and a recipient of a Finalist's Grant from the Massachusetts Cultural Council.

ACE BOGGESS is author of four books of poetry, most recently *I Have Lost the Art of Dreaming It So* (Unsolicited Press, 2018) and *Ultra Deep Field* (Brick Road Poetry Press, 2017,) and the novel, *A Song Without a Melody* (Hyperborea Publishing, 2016). His writing has appeared in *Harvard Review*, *Mid-American Review*, *RATTLE*, *River Styx*, *North Dakota Quarterly* and many other journals. He lives in Charleston, West Virginia.

KATERYNA BORTSOVA's most recent exhibitions include International Artist Grand Prix, X-Power Gallery, Taipei, Taiwan– International exhibition "Lethes Art. Memorty & Identiti(es)", Ponte de Lima, Portugal 2017 – International exhibition "Fire and Ice", Alicante, Spain – Art Revolution Taipei, Taipei, Taiwan, – POČITELJSKA PRIČA, Sarajevo, Bosnia and Hercegovina

MARY LOU BUSCHI's poems have appeared in *Field*, *Willow Springs*, *Indiana Review*, *The Laurel Review*, *Four Way Review*, among others. Mary Lou's full-length collection, *Awful Baby*, was published through Red Paint Hill (2015). *Tight Wire*, her third chapbook, was published by Dancing Girl Press (2016).

BARBARA SIEGEL CARLSON is the author of poetry collections *Once in Every Language* (Kelsay Books 2017) and *Fire Road* (Dream Horse Press 2013), co-translator of *Open: Selected Poems and Thoughts of of Srečko Kosovel* (2018, Tiscarna Present) and *Look Back, Look Ahead, Selected Poems of Srečko Kosovel* (Ugly Duckling Presse, 2010) and co-editor of *A Bridge of Voices: Contemporary Slovene Poetry and Perspectives* (Kindle, 2017). Her poetry and translations have appeared in many journals including *Cortland Review*, *Mid-American Review* and *Salamander*. Carlson serves as Poetry in Translation Editor for *Solstice* and teaches in Boston.

REBECCA CONNORS' poems can be found in *DIALOGIST*, *Menacing Hedge*, and *Tinderbox Poetry Journal*, among others. She is happily settled with her family in Boston, where she is currently an MFA candidate at the Solstice MFA program at Pine Manor College. Her chapbook manuscript, *Split Map*, won the 2018 Dare to Speak contest and will be published by Minerva Rising Press. Follow her on Twitter @aprilist or visit her site at aprilist.com.

SANDY COOMER is an artist and poet living in Brentwood, TN. Her poetry has been published in numerous journals and anthologies and she is the author of three poetry chapbooks and a full-length collection titled *Available Light* (Iris Press). Her art has been featured in local art shows and exhibits and has been published in journals such as *Lunch Ticket,Gravel, The Wire's Dream Magazine, Up the Staircase, Taxicab, Spider Mirror,* and *The Magnolia Review,* among others. Sandy is the director of Rockvale Writers' Colony in College Grove, TN. She is a teacher, a dreamer, a seeker, and an explorer. Her favorite word is believe.

STEVEN CRAMER is the author of *The Eye that Desires to Look Upward* (1987), *The World Book* (1992), *Dialogue for the Left and Right Hand* (1997), Goodbye to the Orchard (Sarabande, 2004)—Sheila Motton Award from the New England Poetry Club and a Massachusetts Honor Book—and *Clangings* (Sarabande, 2012). My poems and criticism have appeared in *AGNI, The Atlantic Monthly, Field, The Kenyon Review, The Nation, The New England Review, The Paris Review, Poetry,* and elsewhere. New work has been published or is forthcoming in *Barrow Street, Bellevue Literary Review, Carolina Quarterly, Massachusetts Review, New Ohio Review, Plume, Salamander,* and *Sugar House Review*. Recipient of a National Endowment for the Arts fellowship, and two fellowships from the Massachusetts Cultural Council, I founded and teach in the Low-Residency MFA Program in Creative Writing at Lesley University.

LISA DESIRO is the author of *Labor* (Nixes Mate, 2018) and *Grief Dreams* (White Knuckle Press, 2017). Her poetry is featured in various anthologies and journals, and has been set to music by several composers. Along with her job as Production & Editorial Assistant for *C.P.E. Bach: The Complete Works,* Lisa is an assistant editor for Indolent Books and a freelance accompanist. Read more about her at thepoetpianist.com

LORI DESROSIERS' poetry books are *The Philosopher's Daughter* (Salmon Poetry, 2013), a chapbook, *Inner Sky* (Glass Lyre Press 2015) and *Sometimes I Hear the Clock Speak* (Salmon Poetry, 2016). A new book of poems, *Keeping Planes in the Air,* will be out in 2020 from Salmon. Her work has been nominated for a Pushcart Prize. She edits *Naugatuck River Review,* a journal of narrative poetry, and *Wordpeace,* an online journal dedicated to peace and justice.

WENDY DREXEL's third poetry collection, *Before There Was Before,* was published by Iris Press in 2017. She's a three-time Pushcart-Prize nominee, and her poems have appeared or are forthcoming in *The Atlanta Review, Barrow Street, Ibbetson Street, J Journal, Nimrod, Prairie Schooner, Salamander, The Maine Review, The Mid-American Review, The Hudson Review, The Threepenny Review, The Worcester Review,* and the *Valparaiso Poetry Review,* among others; featured on *Verse Daily* and WBUR's *Cognoscenti*; and in numerous anthologies. Drexler is currently the poet in residence at New Mission High School in Hyde Park, MA.

SUZANNE EDISON's recent chapbook, *The Body Lives Its Undoing*, was published in 2018. Poetry can be found in: *Michigan Quarterly Review*; *The Naugatuck River Review*; *Isacoustic*; *Persimmon Tree*; *JAMA*; *SWWIM*; *Intima: A Journal of Narrative Medicine*; *The Ekphrastic Review*, and elsewhere. She lives in Seattle and teaches at Richard Hugo House.

KAREN FRIEDLAND lives in the peaceable Boston neighborhood of West Roxbury with her husband, Rich, two dogs and two cats. A grant writer by trade, Karen's poems have been published in *Nixes Mate Review* and *Writing in a Women's Voice*. She has a book of poems forthcoming in summer, 2019 from Nixes Mate Books. Friedland is the interviewer for Cervena Barva Press, and is a founding member of the Boston-based Poetry Sisters collective.

ROBBIE GAMBLE holds an MFA in poetry from Lesley University. His poems have appeared in *Scoundrel Time*, *Writers Resist*, *Stonecoast Review*, *Solstice*, and *Poet Lore*. He was the winner of the 2017 Carve Poetry prize. He works as a nurse practitioner caring for homeless people in Boston, Massachusetts.

JENNY GRASSL was raised in Pennsylvania, and now lives in Cambridge, Massachusetts. Her poems appeared most recently in the *Boston Review* (2018 annual poetry contest, runner-up prize selected by Mary Jo Bang), also in the anthology: *Humanagerie*, (Eibonvale Press, UK), *Ocean State Review*, and *Rogue Agent*. Her poems are forthcoming in: *Massachusetts Review*, *Rhino Poetry*, *Phantom Drift*, and *Radar Poetry*.

ANDREW GUDGEL's poetry has appeared in several volumes of Southeast Missouri State University's *Proud to Be*, and *Asimov's Science Fiction* magazine.

PATRICIA HALE is the author of the poetry collection, *Seeing Them with My Eyes Closed*, and the chapbook, *Composition and Flight*. Her prize-winning poetry appears in many journals and anthologies. She lives in Connecticut and serves on the board of directors for the Riverwood Poetry Series.

YONI HAMMER-KOSSOY's poetry appears in numerous journals and anthologies, including most recently *Stonecoast Review*, *Juniper Poetry*, *Sky Island Journal* and *River Heron Review*. Originally from the US, Yoni has lived in Israel with his family for the last twenty years. When not writing he enjoys hiking, playing Ultimate Frisbee, and would love to open a kosher food truck with friends but alas, still pays the bills as a software engineer.

MARY ANN HONAKER is the author of *It Will Happen Like This* (YesNo Press, 2015). Her poems have appeared in *2 Bridges*, *The Dudley Review*, *Euphony*, *Juked*, *Off the Coast*, *Van Gogh's Ear*, *The Lake*, and elsewhere. Mary Ann holds a BA in philosophy from West Virginia University, a master of theological studies degree from Harvard Divinity School, and an MFA in creative writing from Lesley University. She currently lives in Beckley, West Virginia.

ERIC E. HYETT is a poet, Japanese translator and business consultant from Brookline, MA. Eric's writing appears in magazines and journals; his translation of *Sonic Peace* by Kiriu Minashita was published in 2017 by Phoneme Media and was shortlisted for the National Translation Award and the Lucien Stryk Asian Translation Prize. Eric teaches poetry at PoemWorks: The Workshop for Publishing Poets; memoir writing at the Brookline Interactive Group; and math at Project Place.

CLINTON INMAN, born in England, graduated from San Diego State University where he earned a BA in Philosophy; he is a retired Hillsborough High School English teacher and lives in Florida with his wife, Elba and English Bulldog, Miss Bean.

CHRISTINE JONES is a massage/physical therapist, and an MFA graduate from Lesley University. She's founder/chief-editor of *poems2go*, a public poetry project. Her poetry can be found at *32 poems, Salamander, Crab Creek Review, Naugatuck Review, Cimarron Review,* and elsewhere. She can often be found swimming or surfing alongside her husband near their home in Cape Cod, MA.

PAULA KAUFMAN writes from West Virginia where she dreams of traveling the world or hiking. She is published or forthcoming from *Heartwood, Brittle Star* and *North Dakota Quarterly*.

ANN KENISTON's recent poems have appeared in *Yale Review, Gettysburg Review, Beloit Poetry Review,* and elsewhere. She is the author of a full-length book of poems (*The Caution of Human Gestures,* Wordtech 2005) and a chapbook (*November Wasps,* Finishing Line, 2013), as well as several scholarly books on contemporary American poetry. She lives in Reno, NV, where she is a professor of English at University of Nevada, Reno.

NATASHA KING lives in North Carolina and misses quietly the snows of her childhood. She divides her spare time among the important duties of writing, prowling, and thinking about the ocean.

BETH KONKOSKI is a writer and high school English teacher living in Northern Virginia with her husband and two children. Her work has been published in journals such as: *Story, Mid-American Review,* and *The Baltimore Review*. A second chapbook of her poetry, "Water Shedding" is available from Finishing Line Press.

VERA KROMS authored the chapbook *Necessary Harm,* which was published by Finishing Line press. Her work has appeared in *Gulf Coast, Columbia Journal of the Arts, Tupelo Quarterly, Southern Poetry Review* and elsewhere. She lives in Boston and worked as a programmer for many years.

MERCEDES LAWRY's fiction appears in *Gravel, Blotterature, Cleaver, Gambling the Aisle* and *Thrice Fiction*. She was a semi-finalist in The Best Small Fictions 2016. Her poetry is published in journals such as *Poetry, Nimrod, Prairie Schooner* and others. Her chapbook, "In the Early Garden With Reason" won the 2018 WaterSedge Poetry Chapbook Contest, judged by Molly Peacock and is available on Amazon. Additionally, Lawry has published stories and poems for children.

JENNIFER LOTHRIGEL is an artist and poet residing in the San Francisco Bay area. Her work has been published in *F-Stop magazine, Art Reveal Magazine, Arcturus, Deracine, Rag Queen Periodical, NILVX* and elsewhere. Find her on instagram @PartingMists

MARJORIE MADDOX is a Sage Graduate Fellow of Cornell University (MFA) and Director of Creative Writing and Professor of English at Lock Haven University; Maddox has published 11 collections of poetry—including *Wives' Tales* (Seven Kitchens Press); *True, False, None of the Above* (Poiema Poetry Series and Illumination Book Award Medalist); *Local News from Someplace Else* (Wipf & Stock); *Weeknights at the Cathedral* (WordTech Editions); *Transplant, Transport, Transubstantiation* (Yellowglen Prize; Brittingham and Felix Pollak finalist); and *Perpendicular As I* (Sandstone Book Award— the short story collection *What She Was Saying* (Fomite Press), and over 550 poems, stories, and essays in journals and anthologies. In addition, Marjorie is the co-editor of *Common Wealth: Contemporary Poets on Pennsylvania* (PSU Press 2005), assistant editor of *Presence*, author of four children's books, and the recipient of numerous honors, including Pushcart Prize nominations in poetry and fiction. She gives readings and workshops around the country. For more information and reviews, please see www.marjoriemaddox.com

JENNIFER MARTELLI is the author of *My Tarantella* (Bordighera Press), as well as the chapbook, *After Bird* (Grey Book Press, 2017). Her work has appeared or will appear in *The Sycamore Review, Sugar House, Superstition Review, Thrush*, and *Tinderbox Poetry Journal*. Her prose and artwork have been published in *Five-2-One, The Baltimore Review*, and *Green Mountains Review*. Jennifer Martelli has been nominated for Pushcart and Best of the Net Prizes and is the recipient of the Massachusetts Cultural Council Grant in Poetry. She is a poetry editor for *The Mom Egg Review*.

OCLLO MASON Experiments with acrylic paint to make it move, pop, emerge, and blend in different ways on the canvas. She has been making art for as long as she can remember. The medium of paint has been forever present throughout her journey as an artist. Her current body of work is created with acrylics through a method that never gives the same results twice. This makes the process of creating new works very exciting for the artist. Ocllo is the mother of 3 sons, two of which have left the nest which gives her more time for painting, attending shows and meeting a great community of artists and art lovers.

LIBBY MAXEY is a senior editor at the online journal *Literary Mama*, and she also edits for Amherst College and as a freelancer. Her poems have appeared in *The Fourth River*, *Emrys*, *Think*, *Pilgrimage*, and elsewhere. She reviews others' poetry for *The Mom Egg Review* and *Solstice: A Magazine of Diverse Voices*. Her first collection, *Kairos*, is forthcoming from Finishing Line Press and is the winner of the 2018 New Women's Voices Chapbook Competition. Her nonliterary activities include singing classical repertoire and mothering two sons.

KEVIN MCLELLAN is the author of *Hemispheres* (Fact-Simile Editions, forthcoming), *Ornitheology* (The Word Works, 2018), *[box]* (Letter [r] Press, 2016), *Tributary* (Barrow Street, 2015), and *Round Trip* (Seven Kitchens, 2010). He won the 2015 Third Coast Poetry Prize and Gival Press' 2016 Oscar Wilde Award, and his poems appear in numerous literary journals including *American Letters & Commentary*, *Colorado Review*, *Crazyhorse*, *Kenyon Review*, *West Branch*, *Western Humanities Review*, and *Witness*. Kevin lives in Cambridge, Massachusetts.

MARCY MCNALLY's poetry, short stories, and articles have appeared in numerous print and online publications such as *Willawaw Journal*, *Tiny Spoon*, and *Extreme: An Anthology*.

ELIZABETH MERCURIO is a poet living in Tampa, Florida. She earned an MFA in poetry from The Solstice Low-Residency Program of Pine Manor College. Her work has appeared in, *Third Point Press*, *Philadelphia Stories*, *The Skinny Poetry Journal*, *The Literary Nest*, and *Fledgling Rag*. She was nominated for a Best of the Net award and was the 2016 recipient of The Sharon Olds Fellowship for Poetry.

MICHAEL MERCURIO lives and writes in the Pioneer Valley of Massachusetts. His work has appeared in the *Indianapolis Review* and *Crab Creek Review*. You can find him at poetmercurio.com

RUKHSAR PALLA is currently a graduate student in Emerson College's M.F.A Fiction program. She graduated from Seattle University in 2017 as a Sullivan Scholar where she completed an English/Creative Writing major and a French minor. Her poems have been published in *Fragments*, *The Cape Rock*, *Straight Forward Poetry*, and other literary magazines and journals. She is currently the Fiction Editor of *Redivider*, Emerson College's Literary Publication and the Nonfiction Editor for *Crab Creek Review*, a Washington based literary journal. As President and founder of the Writers of Color Graduate Student Organization at Emerson College, she is working on voicing the collective realities and injustices people of color face, through collective healing and writing-related pursuits. She hopes to graduate from Emerson College in the Spring semester of 2019 with a collection of short stories vocalizing some of the experiences of Pakistani Muslim women globally. In her spare time, she can be found drinking chai next to her pink rose tapestry.

AVI PRAGER is a poet, fiber artist, and alien-dog enthusiast. His work has been featured in The *Raw Art Review*, *The Gateway Review*, and more. Avi never lost his child-like wonder, and loves chaotic wild beauty.

ASHLEY RENSELAER is a ninth grade student at Windward School in Mar Vista, California. She lives in Culver City with her parents and dog and cat and loves writing poems, plays, and short stories. She believes that poetry has the power to change hearts and minds, creating a better world.

SUSAN RICH is the author of five books, most recently, *Cloud Pharmacy*, shortlisted for the Julie Suk prize, honoring poetry books from independent presses. She is the winner of the PEN USA Award for Poetry and the Times Literary Supplement Award, London. Her poems appear in places such as the *Academy of American Poets Poem-a-Day*, *New England Review*, *Southern Review*, and *World Literature Today*. She is cofounder with Kelli Russell Agodon of Poets on the Coast, a yearly writing retreat. She lives and writes in Seattle, WA

STEVEN RIEL's first full-length book of poetry *Fellow Odd Fellow* was published by Trio House Press in 2013. He's also the author of three chapbooks, the most recent of which, *Postcard from P-town*, was runner-up for the inaugural Robin Becker Chapbook Prize and published by Seven Kitchens Press. His poems have appeared in several anthologies and numerous periodicals, including most recently *International Poetry Review* and *Naugatuck River Review*.

BIANCA RIVETTI is an artist and a student for Architecture and Urbanism at the Mackenzie Presbyterian University in São Paulo.

KELLIE SCRANTON is a self-taught artist, who loves every aspect of creativity and strives to create beautiful things to share with the world. She resides in the South Jersey/Philadelphia area. Most of her paintings are done with acrylics, and mixed media components. Her day job is a full time hair-colorist, and she sells original paintings on the side. Check out her Instagram and to see more of her work. She posts her artwork on her personal page (@kelliescranton) her on her art Instagram (@kelliescranton_art)

MELISSA SILVA is a Poet and a Nurse, living in the Boston area. She has studied Contemporary and Asian Poetry, Fiction Writing, and Storytelling/Performance. She is a co-founder of the Poetry Sisters Collective, and was a member of the performing collective Storytellers in Concert, Her poems have appeared in *Tuck Magazine*, *Bonsai*, *Oddball Magazine*, and others. She does promotion for Červená Barva Press, Somerville, MA.

LORI SLAVIN is a former corporate attorney passionately turned abstract painter, and awed by art's capacity to evoke wonder and transformation, even if just for a moment. She strives to bring such experiences to those who view her paintings and creates visual poetry on canvas. For additional information about Slavin's art, please visit lorislavin.com.

*notes vii*

BEN SLOAN teaches at the Fluvanna Correctional Center for Women, the Buckingham Correctional Center, and Piedmont Virginia Community College. *The Road Home*, a chapbook of his writing, is available from Thirty West Publishing House (2017) with more recent pieces appearing in *Streetlight Magazine*, *The Tishman Review*, and *Pembroke Magazine*. His essay entitled "Without Any Constraints: Several Shorter Uncollected Poems by Jonas Mekas in the Company of Aharon Appelfeld" is forthcoming in *Message Ahead* (Rail Editions).

ANDY SMART is a candidate for the MFA at the Solstice Low-Residency Program at Pine Manor College. He lives between the Midwest and New England. His work has appeared in *River Heron Review*, *Two Thirds North*, *Red Fez*, and elsewhere. Andy is an advocate for the de-stigmatization of mental illness, the prevention of suicide, and the continued influence of the written word. He loves every dog he sees.

SARAH DICKENSON SNYDER has three poetry collections, *The Human Contract*, *Notes from a Nomad* (nominated for the Massachusetts Book Awards 2018), and *With a Polaroid Camera*, forthcoming in 2019. Recently, poems have appeared in *Artemis*, *The Sewanee Review*, and *RHINO.*'

MATT STEVENSON is the winner of The Big Snowy Prize in Fiction and has been published in *The Montana Quarterly*, *Cosumnes River Journal*, and *Abstract*.

ANN TAYLOR is Professor of English at Salem State University in Salem, Massachusetts. She has written two books on college writing, academic and free-lance essays, and a collection of personal essays, *Watching Birds: Reflections on the Wing*. Her first poetry book, *The River Within*, won first prize in the Cathlamet Poetry competition at Ravenna Press, 2011. A chapbook, *Bound Each to Each*, was published in 2013. Her most recent collection, *Héloïse and Abêlard: the Exquisite Truth* (2018), is based on the famous twelfth-century story of their lives. She is now working on a new collection of poems, *Sortings*.

CARINE TOPAL'S work has appeared in The Best of the Prose Poem, Greensboro Review, Iron Horse Literary Review, and many other journals. She is the recipient of the Robert G. Cohen Prose Poetry Award, the Briar Cliff Review Award for Poetry and her prize-winning book, Tattooed, won the 4th Biennial Chapbook Contest from Palettes and Quills. Topal's 5th collection, "In Order of Disappearance," was published last year by Pacific Coast Poetry Series.

PETER URKOWITZ has published poems and art in *Meat for Tea: the Valley Review*, *Oddball Magazine*, *Sextant*, and the *Lily Poetry Review*. His *Fake Zodiac Signs* are being published in a forthcoming chapbook from Meat for Tea Press. He lives in Salem, Massachusetts, where he works in a college library.

ANASTASIA VASSOS was born in Cleveland, Ohio and currently lives, writes and teaches in Boston, Massachusetts. Her work has appeared in various journals, including *Gravel Mag, Blast Furnace Press, Haibun Today, The Ghazal Page, Literary Bohemian*, and *Writers Resist*. She was a BreadLoaf General Contributor in Poetry, 2017. Her poem "Tinos, August 2012" was named Poem Of The Moment on MassPoetry.org in 2017. She is a long-distance cyclist.

JESSICA L. WALSH is the author of two collections, *How to Break My Neck* and *The List of Last Tries* (forthcoming spring 2019!), as well as two chapbooks. Her work has appeared in *RHINO, Tinderbox, Rogue Agent*, and more. She teaches at a community college outside of Chicago and manages the blog for Agape Editions.

ElISABETH WEISS teaches at Salem State University. She's taught poetry in preschools, prisons, and nursing homes and as well as to the intellectually disabled. Her poems have appeared in *London's Poetry Review, Porch, Crazyhorse, Ibbetson Street Magazine*, the *Birmingham Poetry Review*, the *Paterson Poetry Review* and many other journals. She was the winner of the Talking/Writing hybrid poetry contest for 2016. A chapbook, The *Caretaker's Lament* was published by Finishing Line Press in 2015.

ROBERT WILSON is a teacher, mentor, and poet living in the Mid-west. His poems have most recently appeared in *Snapdragon: A Journal of Art and Healing*, the *Pinyon Review*, and *Poetica*.

MARGOT WIZANSKY poems have appeared on line and in many journals, such as *The Missouri Review, Crab Orchard Review, Moon City Review, Salamander*, and *The Maine Review*. She edited two anthologies: *Mercy of Tides: Poems for a Beach House*, and *Rough Places Plain: Poems of the Mountains*. In *Don't Look Them In The Eye: Love, Life, and Jim Crow*, she transcribed the oral history of her friend, Emerson Stamps, a grandson of slaves and son of sharecroppers, her poems and his story. Wizansky has recently retired from a career developing housing for adults with disabilities. Margot lives in Massachusetts.

ANTON YAKOVLEV's latest chapbook *Chronos Dines Alone*, winner of the James Tate Poetry Prize 2018, was published by SurVision Books. He is also the author of *Ordinary Impalers* (Kelsay Books, 2017) and two prior chapbooks. His poems have appeared in *The New Yorker, The Hopkins Review, Measure, Amarillo Bay*, and elsewhere. *The Last Poet of the Village*, a book of translations of poetry by Sergei Yesenin, is forthcoming from Sensitive Skin Books.

ART ZILLERUELO's work appears in *Hayden's Ferry Review, The Cincinnati Review, Pleiades, Western Humanities Review*, and other journals. Kattywompus Press published his chapbook *Weird Vocation* in 2015, and Unsolicited Press published his debut full-length collection *The Last Map* in 2017.

www.ingramcontent.com/pod-product-compliance
Lightning Source LLC
Chambersburg PA
CBHW061233070526
44584CB00030B/4103